Land Rover Freelander
Owners Workshop Manual

Martynn Randall

Models covered

(4623 - 336)

Freelander Hardback, Softback & Station Wagon, including special/limited editions
Petrol: 1.8 litre (1796cc) 4-cylinder
Turbo-diesel: 2.0 litre (1951cc) TD4

Does NOT cover models with 2.5 litre V6 petrol engine
Does NOT cover new 'Freelander 2' range introduced November 2006

© Haynes Publishing 2007

ABCDE
FGHIJ
KLMNO
PQRST

A book in the **Haynes Owners Workshop Manual Series**

ISBN **978 1 84425 623 5**

British Library Cataloguing in Publication Data
A catalogue record for this book is available from the British Library.

Printed in the USA

Haynes Publishing
Sparkford, Yeovil, Somerset BA22 7JJ, England

Haynes North America, Inc
861 Lawrence Drive, Newbury Park, California 91320, USA

Haynes Publishing Nordiska AB
Box 1504, 751 45 UPPSALA, Sverige

Contents

you&your
Land Rover
Freelander

you&your
Land Rover
Freelander

James Taylor — *Buying, enjoying, maintaining, modifying*

First published in 2003

A catalogue record for this book is available from the British Library

ISBN 1 85960 899 X

Library of Congress catalog card no. 2003110433

Published by Haynes Publishing, Sparkford, Yeovil, Somerset, BA22 7JJ, UK

Tel: 01963 442030 Fax: 01963 440001
Int. tel: +44 1963 442030 Int. fax: +44 1963 440001
E-mail: sales@haynes-manuals.co.uk
Web site: www.haynes.co.uk

Haynes North America, Inc.,
861 Lawrence Drive, Newbury Park,
California 91320, USA

Printed and bound in England by
J. H. Haynes & Co. Ltd, Sparkford

Jurisdictions which have strict emission control laws may consider any modifications to a vehicle to be an infringement of those laws. You are advised to check with the appropriate body or authority whether your proposed modification complies fully with the law. The author and publishers accept no liability in this regard.

While every effort is taken to ensure the accuracy of the information given in this book, no liability can be accepted by the author or publishers for any loss, damage or injury caused by errors in, or omissions from the information given.

Contents

Introduction and acknowledgements

In one way, this book had to be different from some of the others in the *you & your* series. It is, I believe, the first book ever to be written about the Land Rover Freelander, and so for that reason I thought it was important to establish the background to the range properly before going on to deal with the joys and problems of ownership. So the first part of the book lays out a detailed history of the Freelander – why it was developed, how it was developed, and how it changed in production between the 1998 and 2004 model-years.

Credit where credit is due: I wouldn't have been able to write this book without a great deal of help from Land Rover themselves, who provided information and pictures through their press offices in the UK and USA, and who regularly let me borrow road-test vehicles so that I could maintain a feel for the latest versions of the Freelander. Special thanks there go to Mike Gould, who was UK PR Manager between 1999 and 2002. Land Rover couldn't make them more helpful. On the design and engineering side, Steve Haywood was an enormous help in explaining how the Freelander developed in the early days before production.

I'd also like to pay a special tribute to my colleagues on *LAND ROVER enthusiast* magazine. Martin Hodder must by now be tired of having ideas bounced off him, but he'll be pleased to hear that it's been enormously helpful. Dave Barker has even gone so far as to buy a Freelander himself, and in the long run-up to that decision he tried out a lot, told me what he thought of them, and took some pictures which I've borrowed for this book. Photographer Alisdair Cusick agonised for a couple of years about which Land Rover to buy, and eventually settled on a Freelander too. He hasn't regretted it for a minute. He, too, has been kind enough to let me use many of his top-class pictures in this book.

All sorts of other information has come in from all sorts of other people. I can't list them all here, but they know who they are and here's my chance to say how grateful I am to them. Lastly, if you, the reader, want to add anything to the information in this book (or to correct something I've got wrong), please get in touch through the head office of the publishers. If there's a second edition of the book, I can improve it with what you tell me.

Once you've read this book, you may be insterested in joining the Freelander Club. Find out more about this association of enthusiastic owners at www.freelanderclub.co.uk.

James Taylor
Oxfordshire
October 2003

The World Rally Championship support Freelanders were rebuilt with 2004 front and rear details and demonstrated the model's rally potential to members of the press in 2003.

Chapter One

The need for Freelander

When it was announced in 1997, the Freelander was undoubtedly the most radical vehicle which Land Rover had ever produced. For a company wedded for so long to beam axles and separate chassis frames, to build a vehicle with no chassis and all-round independent suspension required a huge leap of conceptual thinking. Secondly, for a company whose products depend on off-road ability to even think of designing a vehicle without a low range of crawler gears required something akin to a religious conversion. Indeed, the urban, urbane Freelander is a world apart in its intended use from the original vehicle to bear the Land Rover badge – a small and lightweight open pick-up designed primarily as a farmer's runabout, and introduced in 1948.

Perhaps the only thing which these two vehicles have in common is their use of four-wheel drive. There are in fact, many enthusiasts of the traditional Land Rover who still refuse to accept that the Freelander is a Land Rover at all – although many of them will grudgingly admit that it isn't a bad vehicle in itself.

So what happened in the nearly five decades between 1948 and 1997 to make the Freelander a viable commercial proposition? What changes took place in buying habits and buyers' expectations, and what changes took place in the company which owned the right to the Land Rover oval badge? In order to understand that, we have to delve quite a long way back into the past . . .

Origins

If the 1980s were the decade when the four-wheel-drive vehicle became fashionable, the 1990s were the one when reality began to set in.

In the beginning, the idea of driving all of a vehicle's

Opposite: The Freelander is ideal for trail driving, and is seen here in the USA doing just that. (Nick Dimbleby).

road wheels rather than just two of them had been a solution to the problem of maintaining traction and mobility in rough terrain. Indeed, the ancestor of the modern light 4x4 – the Willys Jeep of the Second World War – had been designed as a military runabout which would give soldiers rapid mobility in areas where there were no roads.

When the war ended, the Jeep was quickly adapted to provide similar mobility for farmers as well as doubling as a stationary power source. Not long after that, Rover's Land Rover took up the idea in Britain, and later, Toyota's Land Cruiser did the same in Japan – and so the all-terrain runabout quickly became a familiar part of the civilian motoring scene.

Until the middle of the 1960s, the light 4x4 was always seen as primarily a utility vehicle. Nevertheless,

This is where it all began for Land Rover. Ken Wheelwright's 1949, 80-inch model is a world apart from today's Freelander.

station wagon bodies (beginning with the Jeep Station Wagon of 1946) were made available, and these introduced the idea that the 4x4 utility could also be the basis of a passenger-carrying vehicle.

At this stage, however, the 4x4 station wagon was viewed in the developed world as a special-purpose vehicle; it most certainly wasn't an alternative to a conventional car. By contrast, in the developing territories of Africa and other countries, its ability to carry both passengers and goods across terrain which would quickly defeat an ordinary car meant that it was often bought in preference to such a vehicle. Station wagon variants of light 4x4s were also bought for expedition and safari purposes, where journeys might begin on metalled roads, but would end up in areas where there were nothing more than rough tracks – and sometimes not even that.

So, although the light 4x4 was not an everyday vehicle in the developed countries, it did have a very strong image. First, it was tough: the military used and

abused light 4x4 vehicles, and so did those who drove across the vast plains of Africa where there were no roads. Secondly, it was capable: it could go where ordinary cars could not. In some countries – notably Britain and the USA – there also grew up a 4x4 sporting culture, in which owners would pit their vehicles and their driving skills against apparently impossible terrain. The victor would be the driver and 4x4 which came through fastest, or unscathed.

Around the turn of the 1960s, the American tractor manufacturer, International Harvester, spotted a market opportunity for a new kind of vehicle – one which would combine the ruggedness and go-anywhere ability of the traditional light 4x4 with higher levels of comfort. Thus the farmer would not need to have a utility vehicle for use around the farm and a more comfortable conventional car or estate to take him and his family into town or to tow his caravan. Instead, one vehicle would meet all his needs. It was called the International Scout, and it reached the market in 1961.

Jeep quickly took this innovation on board, and the Jeep Wagoneer, which replaced the elderly Jeep Station Wagon in 1963, was an imaginative assault on the same market. Anxious not to miss out on the action, Ford

The tough image of the modern 4x4 was forged to an extent by its association with the military. This is a Land Rover Ninety belonging to the British Army on exercises in Canada in the early 1990s.

now developed a more compact and manoeuvrable dual-purpose 4x4 called the Bronco. This hit the market in 1965 and Ford's marketing focused on its value as a recreational vehicle – for towing, or for exploring away from metalled roads. All this, combined with the 4x4's existing image of toughness and special-purpose use made an irresistible cocktail. The 4x4 boom had begun.

As the 1960s progressed, Chevrolet joined the fray with their Blazer, while over in Britain the Rover Company's engineers were busily working on a vehicle which would materialise in 1970 as the Range Rover. Jeep gradually refined their Wagoneer to meet buyers' expectations, and by the middle of the 1970s the 4x4 estate car was becoming a common sight in suburban driveways. Buyers were strongly attracted by qualities such as its high driving position (which allowed the driver to see further ahead than in a conventional car), its size and its robustness (which were widely seen as safety factors).

Two things then happened. The first was that Audi developed a 4x4 version of their rather ordinary 100 coupé and started winning rallies with it in 1980. The Quattro quickly became a legend, and suddenly four-wheel drive was the thing to have. Road-testers praised the Quattro's superb traction and handling on the road, too. All this added to the sporting pedigree of cars with all four wheels driven.

The Range Rover, introduced in 1970, probably changed perceptions of the 4x4 more than any other vehicle. This 1988 model, with the then top-of-the-range Vogue SE specification, was photographed by Alisdair Cusick.

By the time of the second-generation Range Rover in 1994, there was a 4x4 luxury class, with price tags to match. Alisdair Cusick's picture shows a 2000 model Vogue variant with the 4.6-litre V8 engine.

The second was that the expanding Japanese motor industry got in on the 4x4 act. The key new arrivals, both announced in 1981, were the Isuzu Trooper and Mitsubishi Pajero (Shogun in Britain). These estates offered all the spaciousness and perceived passive safety of more expensive models like the Range Rover, but sacrificed ultimate rough-terrain ability for more car-like handling on the road. Available in more manoeuvrable short-wheelbase forms with just two

Enormously influential in changing perceptions of 4x4 drivetrains was the original Audi Quattro, introduced in 1980, which made its name as a rally car. This is a later version with the 220bhp five-cylinder engine.

Japanese manufacturers capitalised on the idea of a family 4x4 by introducing Range Rover-like vehicles at lower prices. Among the key models were the Isuzu Trooper (opposite) and the Mitsubishi Shogun (below). Both were available in long-wheelbase four-door form, or as short-wheelbase 'three-doors'.

The diminutive Suzuki SJ was the first really popular 'fun' 4x4 vehicle, combining low running costs and powerful fashion-appeal with excellent off-road ability.

side doors, as well as in family-orientated four-door form, they sold like hot cakes, prompting Land Rover to fight back with the Discovery in 1989.

But the Japanese motor industry had already moved on. This time the key player was Suzuki, who developed a small 4x4 urban runabout called the Jimny (SJ series in Britain) from a more serious 4x4 which they had designed for developing Asian countries at the end of the 1960s. The Jimny was fun, manoeuvrable, and fashionable – and its off-road ability was astounding. Suddenly, 4x4s did not have to be big vehicles with big and thirsty engines any more, and younger buyers who liked the appeal of the 4x4 image could now afford to join in the fun.

Suzuki exploited their advantage, following the Jimny in 1988 with the Escudo (Vitara in Europe), which was similarly compact but offered better road performance from bigger engines and brought more creature comforts and style. Daihatsu had seen the same market opportunity, and announced their Feroza (Sportrak in Britain) alongside the Escudo. Neither the Escudo nor the Feroza excelled in rough terrain, but most of their customers didn't care. These 4x4s were being bought for their go-anywhere image rather than their go-anywhere ability, and few owners ever discovered just how far their vehicles would actually take them across difficult terrain off the road. The motoring press invented a new name to describe them. If the archetypal light 4x4 was an 'off-roader', these were 'soft-roaders'.

By the early 1990s, when 4x4 estates of all sizes were selling profusely, the question being increasingly asked was whether there was any point to all this any longer. What was the use of paying extra for a 4x4 drivetrain when it was never going to be used for the purpose it had been designed for? There was certainly a sort of

Nissan and Ford entered the market with a jointly developed vehicle, badged as Terrano II by Nissan (there had been an earlier Terrano) and as Maverick by Ford. The three-door always had a fixed roof; the five-door aimed upwards at the Discovery and Shogun family market.

Vauxhall's Frontera was actually based on Isuzu models. Some variants overlapped with the Ford Maverick-Nissan Terrano range while others were targeted at the Suzuki Vitara-Daihatsu Sportrak market. The soft-top short-wheelbase Frontera Sport seen here was not a success in the UK; in fact, the author disliked his press-loan vehicle so much that he refused to write about it!

The Toyota RAV4 was a massive success in the later 1990s, combining cheeky 4x4-inspired looks with good road performance. Despite the absence of a transfer box giving low ratios, it was surprisingly competent off-road.

Honda's impressive CRV was the Japanese company's equivalent of the Freelander, offering 4x4 looks with a spacious family orientated interior and very good road performance. Only five-door models were available; there was a very different HR-V model for the three-door 'fun 4x4' market. Honda sponsored the Camel Trophy adventure challenge for a time after Land Rover had withdrawn, and this CRV was decked out for the job.

hypocrisy about the 4x4 boom, although it is important to remember that image played a huge part in the process. The drivers of 4x4s liked the idea that they could go off-road if they wanted to, just as performance car drivers like the idea that they can drive at 180 mph if they wish to. The fact that neither 4x4 driver nor performance car driver ever exploits their vehicles' full potential is simply not relevant.

It was Toyota who broke the mould, with the brave RAV4, initially shown at the 1993 Tokyo Motor Show as a concept vehicle. This was a hugely successful hybrid of conventional 4x4 looks and hot-hatch road

performance and – crucially – it dispensed with a transfer gearbox giving crawler ratios for off-road work. Toyota knew that most customers wouldn't use a transfer gearbox, so they saw no reason to make them pay for one, and it didn't hinder sales one little bit.

Subaru avoided the stereotyped tall 4x4 look, instead adding 4x4 drivetrains to vehicles which looked like conventional cars. The Forester was an excellent road car as well as a good performer in the rough – as long as high ground clearance wasn't needed.

WHO OWNED LAND ROVER?

It is quite important to understand where Land Rover as a company has stood over the years – and there have been major developments even in the few years since the Freelander was introduced to the market.

In the beginning, Land Rover was not a company at all. It was simply a new model, introduced in 1948 by the car manufacturer Rover, and intended to keep the company afloat during the very difficult trading conditions after the end of the 1939–45 war. British companies were encouraged to develop export markets in order to rebuild the national economy, and there was more demand for a lightweight utility vehicle than there was for Rover's traditional middle-class motor cars.

Within three years of the Land Rover's introduction, the new model was out-selling Rover cars by two to one. Without it, Rover would probably have foundered in the 1950s; as it was, profits from Land Rovers shored up the car business and enabled the company to develop the radically new Rover 2000 or P6 model, which was one of the outstanding European cars of the 1960s.

However, changes in the business world forced change at Rover too. When BMC bought out the Pressed Steel Company (which built Rover's bodyshells) in 1965, it initiated a train of events which would lead to Rover's loss of independence. In 1967, Rover joined forces with the Leyland truck and bus group which already owned Standard-Triumph. A year later, government pressure pushed Leyland and BMC (which owned Austin, Morris and other smaller car makers) together in an alliance which eventually became known as British Leyland.

The alliance was never fully cemented, as there was too much rivalry among the companies involved. British Leyland never got to grips with managing its own vast empire effectively, and by the end of 1974, was heavily in debt. The company was nationalised in 1975 in order to save jobs and the bulk of the British car industry.

Re-structuring followed. Land Rover was established as a separate business unit for the first time in 1978, and from 1982 was the sole occupant of the manufacturing site which the Rover Company had occupied at Solihull, Warwickshire since 1945. Although it maintained close links with the car side of the Rover business, which now had its headquarters in the old Austin premises at Longbridge near Birmingham, Land Rover was increasingly becoming a standalone marque.

The British Government, tiring of the British Leyland burden, began looking for a buyer in the mid-1980s. By 1989, it had persuaded British Aerospace to take on what was now known as the Rover Group. But this was always intended as a short-term arrangement, and within five years BAe was looking for a buyer. The Rover Group was sold to BMW, the German car manufacturer, at the start of 1994. The BMW take-over thus occurred during the very early stages of the Freelander project.

The Rover-BMW alliance never worked properly, either. While Land Rover remained profitable, its build quality never matched German expectations, and the Rover Cars side of the business continued to haemorrhage money. By 2000, BMW had had enough. Land Rover was sold to the American giant Ford, and Rover Cars went to a business consortium, emerging shortly afterwards with a fresh image as MG Rover. Under Ford, Land Rover belongs to the Premier Automotive Group of prestige marques, which also includes Jaguar, Volvo, Aston Martin, Mazda, Lincoln and Mercury.

So, when the Freelander was announced in 1997, it looked to most observers as if it was following in the footsteps of the Vitara, the Sportrak and the RAV4. In a way, it was – but the origins of the vehicle which became the Freelander go back much further than most people realise.

After the integration of the Rover Cars and Land Rover engineering departments, which followed the British Aerospace take-over in 1989, there was a great deal of cross-fertilisation of ideas. The project to develop the second-generation Range Rover (launched in 1994) was heavily influenced by this integration, as the 4x4 engineers looked after the drivetrain and off-road performance side of the project while people from the cars side worked on the luxury aspects of the package. The result was a less specialised vehicle, but with a broader appeal than one developed purely by Land Rover engineers would have had – a more truly dual-purpose vehicle than the original Range Rover had been.

By about 1991, the Rover Group as a whole was looking at an emerging market sector which nowadays would be described as a 'crossover' market. The only vehicles which were pointing the way forward then were Suzuki's Vitara and (to a lesser extent) the Daihatsu Sportrak. These offered customers some of the style and image of a 4x4 but were essentially aimed at city dwellers and in that respect were altogether more car-like. 'There was very little competition,' confirms Steve Haywood, who later became chief engineer of the CB40 (Freelander) project. 'We had intelligence to suggest that the Japanese were working on other vehicles of this kind, but there was nothing coming out of the US or Europe.'

It looked like a golden opportunity to get into a developing market at an early stage and become established there before rivals could get in on the act. The next question was whether Rover Group should exploit this market opportunity with a car-type vehicle (which would naturally carry Rover badges) or with a 4x4-type vehicle (which would naturally carry Land Rover badges). So, to take these ideas forward, two separate but related vehicle development programmes were set in train. The car-style project was known as Oden (not Odin, as has sometimes been reported) and the Land Rover-style project was known as Pathfinder.

Both Oden and Pathfinder were taken to the full-size glassfibre mock-up stage. Oden was conceived as a five-door 'tall' estate car (rather along the lines of the Honda Shuttle or Mitsubishi Space Wagon of the time). It would have had two-wheel drive only, with drive to

Suzuki followed the **SJ** with the Vitara, which made the light 4x4 an attractive proposition for fashion-conscious young buyers. More than any other vehicle, this one dictated the market trends in the first half of the 1990s.

the front wheels and an H-frame rear suspension. Pathfinder was conceived as two different vehicles, one a three-door model with a removable rear roof and sides (like the Vitara and Sportrak) and the other a five-door station wagon type of vehicle. Both would have had four-wheel drive, and contemporary photographs show a striking resemblance between the Pathfinder concepts and the eventual production Freelander. Also remarkable is the degree of resemblance between the five-door Pathfinder concept and the Oden concept.

Daihatsu's Sportrak was another important entry into the affordable 4x4 category, sharing many of the Vitara's key elements, but offering a more rugged appeal.

DID YOU KNOW?

Land Rover and Solihull

The Land Rover marque has always been associated closely with the assembly plant at Lode Lane in Solihull which became the home of the old Rover Company in 1945. However, Solihull has not been the only place associated with the Freelander story. Equally important have been Canley (near Coventry) and Gaydon (further south, towards Banbury).

For more than three decades, Land Rover design and development was based at Solihull, on the same site where the vehicles were assembled. However, the early 1980s saw some Land Rover staff moved to other locations, mainly to make room for sub-assembly operations which were being brought into Solihull as some of the older Rover 'satellite' factories in the Birmingham and Coventry areas were closed.

Many of the Rover and Land Rover design staff were moved to the old Standard-Triumph plant at Canley, and it was in fact there that the Freelander was conceived.

Then, in the mid-1990s, the Canley site was closed and its staff, together with those from several other outposts of the Rover Group, moved into purpose-built premises at Gaydon. The Gaydon site was a former RAF base which British Leyland had bought in the 1970s, part of which was converted into a test track at the end of that decade. In 1993, a new museum building opened there as the home of the British Motor Industry Heritage Trust.

Today, Gaydon remains the Land Rover design, engineering and administrative headquarters, while Solihull is the marque's only UK assembly plant. That will change in the next few years, though. The second-generation Freelander will be built at Halewood, on Merseyside.

Seen in the secure 'viewing garden' at Canley are the full-size glassfibre models of Pathfinder (left) and Oden (right). Frontal styling details would have given them very distinct identities, but in many respects the two concepts were very similar indeed . . .

A number of factors steered Rover Group towards the Land Rover rather than the Rover vehicle to fill the perceived market opportunity. A key realisation was that

These are the two glassfibre models seen from the side. The Land Rover proposal is again on the left. Side cladding and the roof bars on the Land Rover make the two models distinctive, but it is quite clear that the basic shape of the Freelander Station Wagon was already in place.

a Land Rover would deliver real off-road ability, and that this was something which the existing and anticipated rivals in the market-place did not have. This off-road ability – whether the buyers ever used it or not – would help to give the vehicle a more distinctive identity and would make it stand out from the crowd. Buyers would also be prepared to pay more for this extra ability, which in turn would lead to larger profit margins.

A second factor at work was admiration for the way BMW had structured its model ranges. The German company – which at this stage had not even considered the idea of buying the Rover Group – had what the product analysts called a 'Life-stage' range structure. It

aimed to capture the young buyer with its entry-level 3 Series models, retain their loyalty when they moved up to a more expensive 5 Series family car, and keep it yet again when (and if) they became senior managers and could afford the luxury 7 Series. Then, on retirement, there were different versions of the 3 Series to retain their lifelong loyalty to BMW.

Land Rover wanted to go this way, too. Its Discovery was (or would become) the 'family' or 5 Series vehicle. Its Range Rover was already the senior manager's equivalent of a BMW 7 Series, but what it lacked was a 3 Series equivalent, which would attract young buyers and would also provide a vehicle for retired buyers. This, then, was an opportunity for Land Rover to develop such a model.

Most important, perhaps, was the recognition that Land Rover technology was relatively old. Every Land Rover had been built on a separate chassis up to this point, but cars had moved over to monocoque bodyshells nearly a quarter of a century ago. There was no experience of weight-saving plastics at Land Rover, and almost no experience of electronic control systems. Integrating these modern technologies into a vehicle which could take the punishment typically given to a traditional Land Rover was a tall order. But if Land Rover was to survive as a marque it would have to move forward.

The decision was then taken that the new model would be a Land Rover, and that as a project it would be used to give the company experience of such things as monocoque bodyshells and electronic control systems within a 4x4 environment. The new vehicle would be an important stepping-stone for the company, and without the experience which it was to bring, vehicles like the third-generation Range Rover (for

which design started in 1996, after BMW had bought the company) would not have been possible.

The group of engineers who had been examining concepts now began to focus on the new vehicle as a Land Rover. There were endless discussions, computer designs, and pieces of paper, but eventually the team – which at this stage had no formal name – decided to put together a concept vehicle which would embody their thinking. And so the Cyclone (see page 20) was built at the tail end of 1993.

'There was a viewing in the design studio at Canley,' remembered Dick Elsy in 1997, 'and the management had come along to review progress on products that were already some way down the road. Anyway, we managed to get the Cyclone into the studio, and kept it covered it up until everybody was deeply engrossed. Then we pulled the covers off it, and the reaction was just electric! John Russell, our sales director, turned round and said: 'I can sell that one now!' So the outcome was that the Rover board gave its approval to further work on the small Land Rover and, as it was my idea, I got put in charge!'

From there to the vehicle which was announced in Autumn 1997 as the Land Rover Freelander was a long hard slog, but the seeds of the idea had been sown. The new vehicle would be developed by Land Rover engineers and would be badged as a Land Rover, and there was no doubt that it would have to embody the Land Rover pedigree and abilities to a very great extent if it was to be worthy of the name.

The three-door version of the Land Rover was modelled on the other side of the glassfibre mock-up. Once again, it's clear that the basic ideas for what would become the three-door Freelander existed long before the project was formally initiated.

THE CYCLONE PROTOTYPE

Although the Cyclone prototype was only a concept vehicle, it was deliberately intended to be something which the members of the Rover board could drive. The idea was that they would be able to get a feel for the vehicle, and to understand what it was intended to be, far better than they would from any styling drawings or static mock-up.

Steve Haywood remembers that it was put together 'in almost no time at all – about four to six weeks at the outside.' To speed up the process, the engineers cannibalised the running-gear from an existing vehicle. This was a red Honda Shuttle – remember that Rover and Honda were collaborating closely at the time and that many Rover cars were re-worked Honda designs. A special body with hand-made monosides was assembled around the Shuttle's running-gear (and the Honda's rear lights were also used to save time), and the result was a 'small, fun, compact, two-door SUV intended to catch the imagination of young buyers. We nicknamed it the Cut-and-Shuttle,' remembers Haywood.

The Cyclone was kitted out with rubberised material on the seats to give a young, contemporary feel, and was painted dark blue.

Stylish side graphics with the Cyclone name completed the picture.

However, this crucial concept vehicle no longer exists. 'It was only really intended as a tease,' according to Dick Elsy, 'to show the sort of thing we had in mind. It was barely driveable! When we moved out of Canley to Gaydon, it was just cut up. You haven't got the space to keep all these things lying around, however much you might like to!'

At the time of the Freelander's launch in 1997, the Cyclone was still something of a touchy subject for Land Rover. The probable reason was that news of its Honda running gear might have caused some embarrassment to a company which was by this stage owned by BMW. In particular, it's important to recognise that Honda as a company had no input whatsoever into the Freelander. Steve Haywood grimaces when he tells the story: 'You wouldn't believe how many people talk to me about Freelander and say, "Ah, but it's only a re-skinned Honda, isn't it?" It isn't!'

This is the crucial Cyclone concept vehicle which kicked the Freelander project into life. Once again seen in the 'viewing garden' at Canley, it was actually based on Honda Shuttle mechanical elements and was driveable.

Chapter Two

CB40 comes together

Although the Oden and Pathfinder concepts had come to an end in 1993, and the way was now clear for Land Rover's new vehicles to begin taking shape, the project was not yet fully established as a production certainty. There was no project team as such, and Project Director Dick Elsy admits to what he calls 'a period of trepidation' during the early part of 1994, when the news broke that BMW had bought the Rover Group.

However, one of the first things which the Germans did was to examine the British company's product portfolio. They looked carefully at the GRP models of the new Land Rover which had been made, they listened attentively to the engineering ideas which were already

in place, and they gave their wholehearted approval. Elsy breathed a sigh of relief and got on with the next stages, which were to present a formal business proposal to BMW in April 1994 and then to assemble a full project team so that the new design could move forward.

Inevitably, there were sporadic reports about friction between BMW and Land Rover after the takeover in January 1994. These were given further fuel by the 1996 statement from BMW Chairman Berndt Pischetsrieder, which condemned Land Rover product quality as unacceptable (which, to be fair, was absolutely right). However, Elsy would have none of that at an interview in 1997. 'The great thing about BMW is that their board

DICK ELSY

Dick Elsy was the project director of the original Freelander programme – the man responsible for oversight of the design and development of the range as it was launched in 1997.

Born in South Shields, Elsy was educated at Durham School and Loughborough University, where he gained an honours degree in engineering science and technology. He started his automotive career at Coventry Climax in 1981 and transferred to Land Rover in 1983. There, he held successively senior appointments until he was put in charge of the CB40 project.

After the Freelander's launch, Elsy was appointed as Product Development Director for the Rover Group, a job which made him responsible for all Rover vehicle development programmes from 1998. That year also saw him presented with the Academy of Engineering Award for his outstanding contribution to British engineering.

However, working in a position of seniority in the Rover Group during its period of BMW ownership carried with it the obligation to live and work in BMW's home town of Munich. Elsy decided that he would rather remain in the UK, and when Jaguar needed a director of product engineering, he applied for the job. His new

appointment was announced in mid-October 1999, and put him in charge of all current and future vehicle and powertrain engineering programmes for the British company.

Project Director Dick Elsy is seen here in the light suit alongside the left-hand headlamp of a three-door Freelander. The picture was taken at the 1997 London Motor Show.

Opposite and above: In the beginning, a team of five designers working with Gerry McGovern was given a free hand to come up with ideas for CB40. These early concepts are quite wild, and one of these, by David Woodhouse, is probably the sketch which inspired the 'Land Rovers of the future' later used in the *Judge Dredd* film starring Sylvester Stallone.

is made up of engineers,' he insisted. 'They know exactly what you're talking about when you present something to them for approval. They are very demanding but also a joy to work with. They're very supportive, and they've taught us real discipline in the achievement of targets.'

The project team assembles

Once BMW had given the new small Land Rover the green light, Dick Elsy began to assemble his team. As his Number Two and the man in charge of engineering, he chose Steve Haywood. Haywood was fresh from an aborted Land Rover project known as Challenger, which had been a plan to engineer future Defender and Discovery models on a common platform. For the styling of the vehicle, Rover Group Design Director Geoff Upex assigned him Gerry McGovern, who had just finished work on the MGF sports car which would be launched in March 1995.

At this stage, the project team was working from offices on the old Standard-Triumph site at Canley near Coventry. This had been the headquarters of the Rover Group engineering and styling teams since the middle of the 1980s, and behind Building 50 (on the main A45 road) was a secure outdoor 'viewing garden' where full-size mock-ups of new vehicles could be assessed. It was here that the pictures in Chapter One of the glassfibre mock-ups of Oden, Pathfinder and Cyclone were taken.

All projects need an identifying name, and the engineers assigned to the new small Land Rover project scratched their heads about the name to adopt. 'We didn't want to call it project Cyclone,' says Steve Haywood, 'because Cyclone had been the concept vehicle and we were designing something new. So we decided to call it after the place where we were based, which was Building 40 at Canley. Putting that together, we came up with CB40.'

There was in fact a precedent within Land Rover for naming a project after the building where its development was based. The second-generation Range Rover was initially developed under the code-name of Project Pegasus, but when the press got hold of that name, Land Rover decided to confuse matters by changing the project

STEVE HAYWOOD

Steve Haywood had been an engineer with Rover Cars before he moved into Land Rovers in early 1991. He took charge of the Challenger project, which was aborted when Land Rover decided to pump resources into the creation of a new small 4x4. As the project team for CB40 was put together, he became its chief engineer under Dick Elsy.

When Elsy moved on some six months after the Freelander had been launched, Steve Haywood was appointed Project Director. He was then moved back to Rover Cars to take charge of Project R30, which was to have been a replacement for the Rover 200 and 400 series ranges. Project R30 was based at BMW's headquarters in Munich, and was cancelled when BMW sold the Rover Group in 2000.

Haywood chose to return to Land Rover and came back to the UK some time around March 2000. He was made Chief Programme Engineer for Discovery and became responsible for overseeing the

Job done! Chief Engineer Steve Haywood with one of the very early production Softback Freelanders.

third-generation (L319) Discovery programme and the model-year upgrades on the then-current Discovery Series II.

name. So Project Pegasus became Project 38A, after Block 38A at Solihull. However, there was no attempt to confuse in the choice of the CB40 name. 'We simply couldn't think of anything else!' remembers Haywood.

The CB40 team was based at Canley for around two years, but by this stage large parts of the old Standard-Triumph site were lying disused and the Rover Group resolved to dispose of it. So towards the end of 1996, the styling and engineering teams were moved into the new purpose-built Rover Group Design and Engineering Centre at Gaydon in Warwickshire. The final phases of Project CB40 were run from there.

Simultaneous engineering

By the early 1990s, the whole of the Rover Group was committed to the simultaneous engineering principles pioneered when the Discovery was being developed as Project Jay in the later 1980s. Simultaneous engineering means that all the design engineers involved with a vehicle can have their say all the way along. It prevents the conflicts and delays which emerged in the traditional design cycle when work done by one department was found to conflict with another department's plans only after it had been completed.

The basics of CB40 were quite clear by the early summer of 1994. It would have a monocoque body with all-round independent suspension carried on sub-frames. Both of these design characteristics represented radical breaks with Land Rover tradition, and there was a lot of resistance within the company to taking Land Rover down this route. 'We were regarded as a bunch of mavericks,' remembers Steve Haywood.

The idea of making CB40 two vehicles was still in the

Opposite and below: These two concepts are distinctly more sober and realistic, and represent a later stage in the design process. They show clearly how the three-door and five-door models were intended to have very different appeals.

plan. One would be a three-door convertible model aimed at the younger and image-conscious buyers of the three-door Vitara and its ilk. The other would be a five-door estate aimed at the family buyer and intended to poach customers from the conventional estate-car market as well as from the cheaper five-door Japanese 4x4s. Like the Land Rover Discovery, they would be based on the same wheelbase of around 100 inches. This would bring valuable savings in manufacturing costs because it was possible to use a greater number of common components. The Japanese approach was (and still is) to build three-door and five-door versions of the same model on different wheelbases.

Stylist Gerry McGovern had already done a lot of work to tidy up the basic shapes which had been

GERRY McGOVERN

Gerry McGovern had joined the Rover Group in the mid-1980s and had been responsible for some striking concept vehicles which were badged as Rovers and MGs. He was responsible for the looks of the acclaimed MGF announced in 1995 – but before that model became public knowledge he had already moved on to the CB40 project as its chief designer.

McGovern was later head-hunted for Lincoln in the USA by Wolfgang Reitzle, the BMW man who had been put in charge of the Rover Group immediately after the German company's takeover of Rover and Land Rover. When Reitzle was out-voted by a BMW board keen to divest itself of the British companies, he moved on to Ford, where he took charge of the Premier Automotive Group to which Lincoln belonged.

Designer Gerry McGovern (left) is pictured here with Geoff Upex, design director for the Rover Group, outside the company's Gaydon headquarters. Behind them, the three-door Freelander appears to have a colour-coded hardback – but this is actually a trick of the light.

LAND-ROVER

Britain's Most Versatile Vehicle

conceived in pre-CB40 days, and in particular he had endowed them with a chunkier appearance which suggested the ruggedness of the Land Rover beneath. The van-like profile of early three-door designs had gone, and the five-door now sported a small step in its rear roofline which was designed to reinforce a family resemblance to the larger Discovery. Perhaps most notable within McGovern's contribution to CB40 was the muscular appearance of the front end, with its deep apron, strong vertical bars beside the air intake grille and high-set headlights.

Meanwhile, Land Rover stylist Memo (Mehmet) Ozoturk had been working on the interior design. Ozoturk was part of McGovern's team and not part of

Getting closer to the design adopted for production are these sketches showing the three-door model, now with its distinctive sloping rear window pillar which had been envisaged in the days of the Pathfinder concept.

DID YOU KNOW?
The Freelander name

Before the official announcement of the new Land Rover, there was speculation in the press that it would be called the Highlander. However, the rights to that name had been owned by Volvo for many years and there was never any chance that Land Rover would have used it.

The Freelander name was on a short list of 'possibles' under consideration for quite a long time, but the final choice wasn't made until a few months before the press introduction in 1997.

Alternative front-end designs were being tried when this full-size clay model was photographed . . .

. . . and the full-size clay below is close to the finished article, but has an uneasy, van-like appearance at the back.

The next stage was a series of full-size glassfibre models. Pictured in the outdoor viewing area at Canley, this one shows some interesting proposals which were not adopted: look at the headlights, the side bump-strip and the grey-coloured sloping rear pillar, for example.

Blacking out the rear pillar on the three-door served to emphasise the van-like rear view, and the idea was abandoned after this full-size glassfibre model had been built.

This full-size glassfibre model of the five-door model shows some interesting front-end differences from the production model, and has a nagging resemblance to the Honda CRV. Note how the side door windows are blacked out.

MARKET RESEARCH

To gain an in-depth understanding of customer motivations and needs, Land Rover carried out major research programmes in its key world markets.

These began with interview sessions in Germany, Italy, Australia and Britain, with existing owners of key small and medium 4x4 vehicles. The objective was to obtain a realistic picture of the rational and emotional appeals of these vehicles, and to see if these varied significantly across these sample markets.

Among its many interesting findings, this exercise revealed that these vehicles had substantially greater appeal to women drivers than larger 4x4 vehicles, with females making up some 40 per cent of respondents. It also showed that over 80 per cent of owners had no previous experience of a 4x4 – a factor which had a major impact on the design priorities of the Freelander. Once people had experienced motoring with a small or medium 4x4, they tended to be loyal to their choice, with 70 per cent saying that their next vehicle would be in this category. The reasons for purchase gravitated around the vehicles looking 'different', having a rugged image, being roomy and comfortable, and able to cope safely with all conditions.

Other international market research activities included product clinics at which three-door and five-door design models were shown to selected potential customers. These confirmed that the strategy of producing two versions of distinctly different character and image off the same basic platform was successful, particularly in terms of covering a wide span of the small-and-medium 4x4 leisure market. For, in addition to having size as a differentiator, this market had become quite intricately fragmented, with products falling broadly into three groups: Traditional (e.g. Jeep Wrangler), Family (e.g. Nissan Terrano) and New Wave (e.g. Toyota RAV4).

Overlaid on these broad groupings were other image dimensions, such as masculine vs feminine, rounded vs square, and mass brands vs 4x4 specialists.

Respondents' perceptions of the Freelander models were that they were solid, rounded and modern 4x4 vehicles. The three-door clearly conveyed an image of fun, youthfulness, urban orientation and versatility for multiple uses. By contrast, the five-door was seen as something new, of serious intent, appealing to families and older, more conservative users, and with a more out-of-town character.

One particularly strong message which came through was that there were many male buyers who had considered moving into the small or medium 4x4 sector, but who had held off because they could not find what they considered to be a 'serious' product with the right kind of pedigree. There was a corresponding enthusiasm for the suggestion that Land Rover might enter this sector. The brand was very well recognised and respected; it was seen to be the ideal stamp of authenticity for a new product with car-like driveability and refinement.

The average age of the compact 4x4 buyers surveyed was 38, but this derived from a very broad spread of ages, from under 20 to over 50. Although this type of vehicle tends to be associated with young couples or single professionals, it has a significant role with young families and the 'young at heart' of any age.

the CB40 core team, and he had started by suggesting strongly contrasting interior themes for the three-door and five-door versions of CB40, to emphasise the difference in their characters. As is the way with such things, the realities of production complication and manufacturing cost brought the two interiors much closer together than originally envisaged. Nevertheless, there would be noticeable differences between the two vehicles' interiors despite the use of many common components.

The exterior and interior styling were signed-off in November 1994. It was then up to the engineers under Steve Haywood to finish development of the structure and the mechanical components. The CB40 team had a target date of Autumn 1997 for a start to production, which would then be ramped up to full volume by the time the first vehicles went out to Land Rover showrooms in January 1998.

The bodyshell

Even though the principles of simultaneous engineering remained in place throughout, development of the driveline was separated from development of the body because the two proceed at different paces. In charge of the monocoque's development was Mark Burniston, who used CAD/CAM technology in the initial stages of the design. 'We then built some bodyshell simulators over the summer of 1994 to validate the analysis tools we had programmed into the computers,' he explained. 'We still had a big crash problem at that stage, but we were able to sort it out quite quickly. It's really a case of spreading loads, both to prevent stress deformation and to give good collision performance. We'd got it right by February 1995, when we achieved a really good offset-frontal crash performance.'

From then on, work concentrated on refining and improving bodyshell detail. Burniston remembered the

This is an early design concept sketch for the interior.

Useful stowage spaces had given the Discovery great appeal, and the Land Rover designers incorporated similar ideas into CB40. This sketch shows the underfloor stowage box at the rear.

Above and below: These interior design theme sketches show attempts to make the three-door and five-door models very different from one another. In production, the two were much closer together in design.

cut-off points he was given. 'August 21st, 1995 was etched in my brain as the cut-off date for the five-door shell,' he recalled with a grin. 'After that, we couldn't make any improvements because the production tooling was being made. The three-door cut-off was a little bit later, in October. I won't pretend that either of them is a production manager's dream, because we did have some arguments about the way we wanted certain things to be made. But in the end we had to make the bodyshells do a job, and we couldn't compromise on safety levels, which were set at the level of US standards.'

There was no argument about the torsional stiffness of the bodyshells which resulted. The average for a saloon

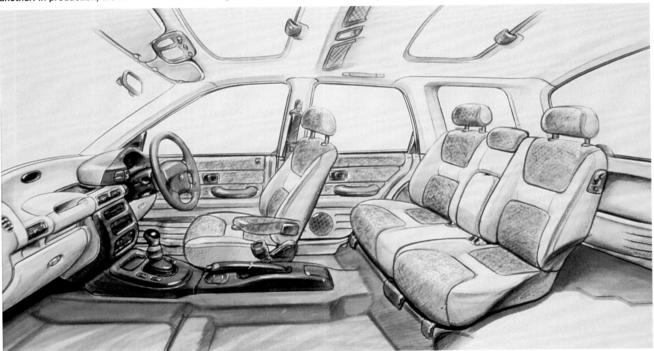

car's monocoque at the time was 10,000Nm per degree; the three-door Freelander's monocoque had a stiffness of 13,500Nm per degree, and that of the five-door was 17,500Nm per degree. These results were a fundamental factor in making Freelander drive more like a car than any other 4x4 on the road when it was new.

The driveline

Right from the beginning, a decision had been taken that CB40 needed modern engines (which ruled out anything in the Land Rover arsenal) and that it should use variants of existing or planned car engines (because the cost of developing unique engines would have been prohibitive).

This automatically meant that all of CB40's engines would be transversely installed, as in all Rover's then-current front-wheel drive cars, rather than north-south, as in all other Land Rover products. The implication of this was that none of the existing Land Rover engines could ever be used in CB40 without substantial and expensive re-engineering – for which, read that it would never happen.

The choices almost made themselves. Under development since 1992 had been the L-series 2-litre direct-injection turbodiesel, initially planned for 1994 introduction in the Rover 600 saloon, but obviously tuneable for a Land Rover application. In addition, a 1.8-litre edition of the latest K-series petrol engine was being developed for Rover saloons and for the MGF sports car.

DID YOU KNOW?
Canley Building 40

The Freelander's project code-name of CB40 was taken from the name of the building where it was being developed – Canley Building 40.

Canley Building 40 was originally built up in 1936–37 with a large factory floor area attached to it, as part of the government's 'shadow factory' programme. It was destined to build Claudel Hobson aircraft carburettors during the Second World War.

After the war, the factory floor became a massive Standard-Triumph machine shop, and also housed assembly of engines and transmissions for cars and Ferguson tractors. Part of it also became a spares warehouse. The office blocks became the headquarters of Standard-Triumph's sales and marketing divisions, and of the parts operation.

After car assembly closed down in 1980, the factory part was mothballed, and before long the buildings themselves were demolished. However, the offices, close to the main A45 road, were retained. During their time as the Austin-Rover (and later Rover Group) headquarters, they contained a studio and a secure outdoor 'viewing garden'.

Meanwhile, work had started on a massive new technical centre at Gaydon, on the site of the old RAF V-bomber base which British Leyland was already using as its test track. By the end of 1996, everyone in the Canley CB40 complex had relocated to Gaydon, and the Canley buildings were demolished.

Much of the old Canley site has been redeveloped as a shopping centre, but at the time of writing there were no new buildings on the old CB40 site.

DID YOU KNOW?
Winning over the die-hards

When the Freelander was launched in 1997, Project Director Dick Elsy made no bones about the fact that 'there were some die-hards in the business who worried about the engineering solutions we were working on in the beginning. But I'm pleased to say that they were amazed by the performance of the prototypes, and converted to our way of thinking. In fact, some of them are now the loudest advocates of what we've achieved with Freelander!'

One of those who raised serious doubts was Land Rover's Demonstrations Manager Roger Crathorne. Hugely respected as an off-road driver and driving instructor, Roger had joined Land Rover in 1964 and had worked his way up through the company, spending a period on the original Range Rover project and being assigned to an overseas regional manager's job for a while. By the time Freelander was launched, Roger was completely converted to the new vehicle, and Steve Haywood remembers how his change of heart came about.

'We went down to Eastnor Castle with one of the Maestro van prototypes, and I took Roger out round the off-road circuit with a Defender 110 as back-up vehicle, just in case! When we'd finished, Roger was just bubbling over with enthusiasm for the vehicle's performance. Of course, it was much lighter than a traditional Land Rover, so it didn't get bogged down as easily, and we had Hill Descent Control and Electronic Traction Control on it as well. It tackled everything we threw at it!'

These two would be made available for CB40 from the beginning and, later, a version of the 2.5-litre KV6 powerplant unveiled in the 1996 Rover 800 would also go into production. Indeed, a look under the bonnet of the Freelander made it quite clear that the vehicle had been designed to accept this engine from the outset. The 1.8-litre petrol and 2-litre diesel engines looked quite lost in an engine bay designed to accommodate the physically much larger Rover V6.

'I argued very strongly for inclusion of the V6,' remembers Steve Haywood, 'but we didn't get the support from North America that we needed.' Land Rover North America took the view that CB40 was too small for potential buyers across the Atlantic. As the bigger and thirstier engine would only have accounted for a small proportion of sales in European markets where fuel is much more expensive than in North America, likely sales volumes were too small for Land Rover to absorb the cost of putting the model into production.

However, Haywood made sure that the V6 was 'package protected' – in other words, that the CB40 engine bay was designed to be big enough to take the V6 engine if there was a later change of heart; and indeed there was. Just a couple of years later, in 1996, Land Rover North America decided that it could find customers for a Freelander with a V6 engine, and so work began in earnest to develop that model. A fuller explanation of what happened is in Chapter 5.

Essentially, development of the L-series and K-series four-cylinder engines for CB40 revolved around re-tuning them to give more low-down torque. In some cases, ancillaries also had to be repositioned to keep them out of the way of the water and mud thrown up in typical off-road driving. The diesel engine's turbocharger had to be changed and mounted more rigidly before it was suitable for the very different environment in which an off-roader's engine has to live. Land Rover knew, of course, that most CB40 owners would probably never venture off-road; but they also knew that if the vehicle were to be found lacking by those who did, it would do incalculable harm to the Land Rover image.

So, CB40 had to have a credible off-road performance. The independent suspension was carefully designed with that in mind, and the whole 4x4 drivetrain was designed so that CB40 would out-perform any competitive vehicles in its market sector. If the transfer box had to be deleted – 'it confused people and added weight', as one engineer explained to me – CB40 still had to have the low-speed mud-plugging and hill-descending ability of its stablemates. Therefore, the engineers came up with an ingenious system which operates through the ABS to ensure that traction is available at all times. It was so good that BMW later borrowed one element of it – Hill Descent Control (HDC) – for their own sporty 4x4 vehicle, the X5.

Mules and prototypes

Driveline and suspension had been developed to an advanced stage long before the bodyshell was ready, and Land Rover needed to test them in real-life conditions as quickly as possible. In late 1994, CB40 mechanical underpinnings were dressed up with the bodies of Austin Maestro vans and sent out on the

Once the first proper prototypes took to the roads, Land Rover resorted to various different disguises to deflect attention. This Station Wagon was unbadged, had an 'old' registration number and was painted an uninteresting-looking military khaki.

THE 'MAD MAX' VANS

The 'Mad Max' vans were the first CB40 prototypes – in fact engineering 'mules' with CB40 drivelines and suspension built into Maestro van bodies. There were 22 of them, built in late 1994 and all painted black. Their registration numbers came from a collection of unrelated numbers allocated to the Rover Group, and were all traceable to issuing authorities well away from Land Rover's Midlands home.

These prototypes were used for over 350,000 miles of road, mixed terrain, high-speed and off-road durability testing. Their disguise meant that they did not have to be restricted to proving grounds or the hours of darkness. They allowed initial powertrain and chassis systems development to be done, and permitted realistic evaluation of driving characteristics both on and off the road.

Some of these vans were identified correctly for what they were while out on the roads during development testing, and some motoring magazines published 'scoop' photographs. However, the disguise was so effective that the photographs revealed absolutely nothing of any value. All that

The rear view of one of the Maestro van 'Mad Max' mules. Both vehicles in these pictures had registration numbers which suggested they were already five or six years old, to help deflect attention while they were out on the roads. Some examples had complete Freelander interiors as well.

could be seen were a high ground clearance and a transverse rear silencer! A closer look would actually have revealed a little more, as some of these vehicles also had proper CB40 dashboards and seats.

According to Dick Elsy, Rover Group headquarters also fielded a number of phone calls from members of the public, asking where they could buy 'one of those four-wheel-drive Maestro vans'!

Rover had probably used the Maestro van disguise before. A few years earlier, a white vehicle with widened wheelarches caught by a 'scoop' photographer was said to have concealed the drivetrain of the Pathfinder, the small 4x4 which Rover Group was thinking about before the CB40 project came into being.

You probably wouldn't have given this van a second glance if you had seen it on the roads in the mid-1990s – and that was the idea. Underneath the Maestro van body is a full set of prototype Freelander running gear.

When Land Rover needed a test mule for the Freelander's tail door with its electrically-operated glass, a prototype version was built into a Discovery. The vehicle was then badged as a Honda Crossroad (the badge-engineered Discovery sold in Japan), to confuse those who saw it on the roads.

The disguise worked; the author spotted it on the M40 one day long before the Freelander launch and followed it at speed, but was unable to work out what it was!

The Freelander tail door with its automatic glass lifting mechanism was built into this Discovery for test purposes, and the vehicle was then badged as a Honda Crossroad (the badge-engineered Discovery sold in Japan). Here it is at the Freelander technical seminar held at Gaydon on 16 July 1997.

roads and test tracks. 'We called these the 'Mad Max' vans,' remembered Steve Haywood. The name came from the *Mad Max* film, and all these vans were painted black to avoid attracting undue attention.

Testing of the prototype vehicles took place around the globe. Here are unbadged three-door models – a RHD Hardback and a LHD Softback – outside the test HQ in the Australian Outback. Like all the prototype vehicles, they carried registration numbers which made them look older than they were and could not be traced to Solihull.

'One of the big problems at the Maestro van stage was propshaft noise,' explained refinement engineer Mike Veal at the Freelander Technical Seminar held for journalists in July 1997. 'We had a sliding spline on the shaft, and we were getting noise through the centre bearings. So we went for a GI joint very early on. The front propshaft also has a larger diameter than the rear, again for refinement reasons. And we got a driveline vibration early on, which we finally solved about six months ago by fitting a big torsional absorber just behind the VCU. We changed the clutch for the same reason.'

Early in 1995, bodyshell development had caught up with driveline work, and so the CB40 team proceeded to the next stage. This was the construction of six hand-made Specially Engineered Prototypes (SEPs). There then followed a main prototype batch of 56 vehicles, beginning in September 1995. These were what the engineers referred to as the '002' phase vehicles – the last ones built before production tooling was made. They went into an intensive test programme which was conducted both at home and overseas.

'We test worldwide, on all five continents,' explained Dick Elsy. 'We have to chase the weather. If we need to do our hot-weather testing when it's winter over here, we have to ship the vehicles out to Australia to do it!' So to Australia some of the prototypes went during the winter of 1995–96. 'We also involved our overseas markets, like Australia, in this phase of the vehicle's

One of the Australian test prototypes is pictured in typical conditions in the outback. The picture dates from January 1997 – the height of the Australian summer when, of course, it was cold and miserable back home in the UK.

Above: More rough-road and hot-climate testing was done with prototypes in southern Africa. This five-door model – unbadged and with misleading zigzag decals on the rear flanks – was pictured on the border with Swaziland by Chief Engineer Steve Haywood.

Below: This second view of the southern Africa test Station Wagon shows how little disguise was used. There is blackout masking around the main lamp units, and an A-frame bull-bar conceals the grille, but that is all.

Above: By the time this Freelander went on test in Oman, Land Rover was no longer concerned about concealing its identity and it wore full badging. However, the five-spoke wheels were not production items. Oman and Dubai provided the outside temperatures to test the air-conditioning system, while the black paint provided a worst-case heat-absorption scenario.

Below: Several early production vehicles went through crash tests to ensure that the real-life performance lived up to the computer's predictions. This Softback – number 600211 – was subjected to an offset frontal crash test at MIRA.

FREELANDER PROTOTYPES

Land Rover built more than 200 Freelander prototypes . . .

The first CB40 prototypes were the 'Mad Max' Maestro vans (see page 33). These were known as 'Simulator' vehicles, and there were 22 of them.

Next came another 62 vehicles which closely resembled the finished article and were built from low-volume prototype tooling. This is very much cheaper to make than cast steel production tooling, but is made of aluminium and resin and wears out after stamping a few hundred pressings.

Those 62 vehicles were built in two groups. The first group of six were Specially Engineered Prototypes (SEPs) and were built by hand in early 1995. Three of them had diesel engines and three had petrol engines.

Build of the second group began in September 1995. There were 56 of these, a figure which included at least one example of each derivative planned to be available at the sales launch. These were the 'DO2' prototypes, and they were used for early validation and development work, including crash testing.

The next stage vehicles were known as the 'D1' prototypes, and they were the first ones built from pressings made on production tooling and assembled in the dedicated assembly hall at Solihull. Their assembly began in July 1996, and the sign-off tests were all done on these. Of the 127 vehicles in this group, 50 went straight into the crash-test programme (some Rover Group sources have claimed there were actually 160 D1 prototypes in total). Others went to the chassis development engineers, the reliability testers, the electrical development engineers, and so on.

The final stages – pilot-production or pre-production vehicles rather than prototypes – were further groups of Freelanders built on production tooling and known as the QP and QC vehicles. The QP (Quality Proving) group were used to check the manufacturing processes, and the QC (Quality Confirmation) group were a final check that all was well before volume production began.

Where are they now?

Most prototypes of any new vehicle are either destroyed in testing or are sent to the crusher after their useful experimental lives are over. No manufacturer will nowadays risk letting one get into private hands for fear of a hugely expensive lawsuit if the owner is injured in an accident resulting from the failing of an incompletely developed vehicle.

Nevertheless, a few Freelander prototypes still exist. Two of the Maestro van 'mules' are currently on loan to the Dunsfold Collection of Land Rovers (although Land Rover retains ownership of them). A small number of the early models made on production tooling have also survived in company hands. At least one now belongs to the Heritage Motor Centre's museum collection at Gaydon in Warwickshire.

development,' said Elsy. 'That proved invaluable. It builds up trust between the sales people and the manufacturer, and they can inject all sorts of ideas and criticisms that we wouldn't have thought of back here in Warwickshire.'

Further testing was carried out in South Africa, Dubai and Oman, where the hot climate, dusty environment and rough roads subjected the CB40 prototypes to the worst possible conditions as the Land Rover engineers tried to discover any weaknesses. In these countries, where the vast open spaces do not encourage 'scoop' photographers to lie in wait for prototype vehicles out on test, the CB40s mostly ran without disguise – although they were unbadged.

Cold-climate testing was done in Alaska and northern Europe, which is a favourite hunting-ground for such photographers, and so the vehicles usually wore disguise panels. Similar panels were also used when there was any risk of a prototype being photographed in the UK and in the west of Ireland. On the whole, though, the engineers preferred to dispense with the plastic cladding which concealed the true shape of what was underneath. 'It gives you a false impression,' explained Steve Haywood. 'You can't tell if there's a wind noise problem, you get high underbonnet temperatures because the panels restrict the airflow, so you're not really testing the intended production design'

Meanwhile, over the summer of 1995, work had also begun on the construction of the new assembly plant at Solihull – 'before we'd built any proper prototypes, please note!' said Elsy with a grin. In fact, the plant was created on computer before any building work was done, and computer-generated graphics enabled the manufacturing people on the CB40 team to watch the vehicle being built, stage by stage, before any real vehicles existed! Investment and support from BMW enabled Land Rover to build a far better assembly hall than originally planned for CB40, and the building was completed by July 1996.

It was here that the final batch of prototypes was built, this time consisting of 127 vehicles made from production tooling. Further testing followed, and once all the test data had been fed back into the system and final adjustments had been made, the new assembly hall began turning out the first production vehicles. Among them were the ones which would form the press fleet that journalists would be able to test on the worldwide media launch of Freelander in Spain, a few months after the new vehicle's public introduction at the Frankfurt Motor Show on 9 September 1997.

Chapter **Three**

Freelander revealed

Press speculation about the forthcoming new Freelander had been so intense that Land Rover decided to release a picture of the genuine article early on. The first media release was on 18 March 1997 – about 10 months before the vehicle would actually go on sale. Not immediately obvious at the time was that the pre-production vehicles in the picture released lacked some of their production badging – it was simply not ready in time!

Next in the pre-launch programme was a special press briefing at the Rover Group's brand-new engineering headquarters at Gaydon on 16 July. Those of us who attended what Land Rover billed as a 'technical seminar' were not disappointed.

The very first press picture of the Freelander was issued in March 1997. A magnifying glass will show that the pre-production Softback on the left has no Freelander badge on the tail door.

This three-door bodyshell was on display at the press briefing held at Gaydon in July 1997. Note the strong longitudinal rails and the hefty cross-members integral with the floorpan.

DID YOU KNOW?
Monocoque 4x4s

Traditionally, road vehicles had always been based on a strong load-bearing chassis, typically of ladder-frame construction, to which a body structure had been mounted. Monocoque structures – where the vehicle is essentially a large metal box and has no separate underframe – began to appear in the 1930s and were almost universal for cars by the end of the 1960s. However, large commercial vehicles and 4x4s still usually had chassis frames because these enabled their structures to absorb greater shock-loadings than monocques of the time could handle.

The first monocoque 4x4 available to the public was the Russian-built Lada Niva, introduced in 1978. This was followed by the American Jeep XJ range (mostly badged as a Cherokee) in 1983. While the short-wheelbase Niva was very successful in engineering terms, the longer distance between the Jeep's axle centres could expose torsional weaknesses in the structure in certain circumstances.

It was advances in structural engineering brought about by computer-aided design which allowed Land Rover to trust a monocoque for the Freelander. Five years later, the company would be confident enough of monocoque structures to use one for the third-generation Range Rover – a much bigger and heavier 4x4 than the Freelander.

Centre of the event was a large ground-floor hall where Freelander prototypes, pre-production vehicles, bodyshells and mock-ups had all been laid out for the press to inspect. In the rooms leading off that main hall were displays which had been put on by individual engineering teams who had been involved in the project. Some showed elements of the body design – and journalists were invited to walk on a Freelander front wing to show how its composite construction resisted damage and deformation – while others showed elements of the engineering such as door lock design, engine and transmission design, and so on. Above all, the design engineers themselves were there, and only too willing to answer questions about their new baby. It was a golden opportunity to find out what made the new Freelander tick.

Structure

That Freelander had to have a monocoque body rather than the traditional Land Rover ladder-frame chassis and separate body had been evident from early on. The traditional Land Rover was a large machine, and quite forbidding in appearance to those used to conventional small cars. So if the new Land Rover was to appeal to such people, it would also have to be smaller than earlier examples of the breed. If its running costs were not to be an obstacle, it would have to have smaller and more economical engines, and its bodyshell would have to be relatively light in weight. A monocoque structure was the only way of satisfying all these requirements.

However, the monocoque had to be unusually resistant to bending forces, because if the new model was to perform Land Rover-style off the road, it would be subjected to torsional forces far above those imposed on any normal car. So the designers made sure that the monocoque was very stiff indeed. Underneath, they gave it two full-length longitudinal box-section members made of high-strength steel and coupled one to the other by eight cross-member units. In plan, they resembled a conventional ladder-frame chassis. To these were welded the main body structure – and below them were mounted separate front and rear sub-frames which carried the vehicle's running-gear.

All Land Rover products up to this point had featured body panels made of aluminium alloy (although the stress-bearing roof of the Discovery and certain other panels had been made of steel). The Freelander's bodyshell thus broke with tradition in being made of steel with mainly steel outer panels. To guarantee the rust-resistant longevity for which Land Rovers were famous, the steel was coated on both sides with zinc.

However, not every outer panel was made of steel. The front wings, as already noted, were made of a

Very early Freelanders are seen here on the assembly lines at Solihull. Clearly visible in this picture are the transverse rear silencer and the spare wheel mounting structure which also carries the arm for the third brake light. The Land Rover name was featured no fewer than three times on the rear of the vehicle – moulded into the bumper, on the moulding above the numberplate, and on the lens of the third brake light.

composite plastic material which resisted deformation and would spring back into shape after light nudges – typically caused by misjudging a distance at low speed in a car park. The front and rear bumpers, moulded in one with the aprons, were made of impact-resistant colour-impregnated plastic. To complete the body's protective armour, each wheelarch carried a protective extension made of the same impact-resistant material. These were a deliberate visual reminder of the wheelarch 'eyebrows' which were a feature of the utility Defender range, and which had been introduced on the first of the coil-sprung Land Rovers – the One Ten – back in 1983.

Exterior styling

Gerry McGovern, the man responsible for the Freelander's visual appearance, hated the word 'stylist'.

There had been great attention to detail in the design of the Freelander. Even the fuel filler cap had been carefully styled.

As far as he was concerned, he was a 'designer', and he had designed the Freelander to fit in with a number of specific requirements.

Making it look fresh and appealing to car buyers while retaining visual links with the established Land Rover models had been a particular challenge. The front-end design had been drawn up to give an impression of strength which McGovern saw as an essential Land Rover characteristic, and he had tried to convey this message through the deep bumper-and-apron assembly, the powerful vertical bars on either side of the grille, and the set-back headlamps. But to reinforce the Land Rover family appearance, he had given the bonnet a hint of the castellations – raised outer ends – which had for so long been characteristic of the Range Rover.

At the rear, the pillar-mounted lamp units with their circular inserts were deliberately designed to resemble the circular rear lamps traditional to Land Rover utilities. Meanwhile, the horizontal indicator and tail lamp units set into the rear bumper were designed as an echo of the Discovery, as facelifted in 1994. They were actually a neat solution to a problem highlighted by the earlier versions of the Discovery, which had all their lights mounted in the pillars: when the side-hinged rear door was open, only one set of lights could be seen from some angles. Fearful of contravening the increasingly difficult US traffic regulations, Land Rover had moved the lights before selling Discoverys in North America.

Also deliberately designed to remind observers of the Discovery was the hint of a stepped roofline in the five-door models, known by the traditional Land Rover name of Station Wagons rather than by the conventional car description of estates. Roof bars on both three-door and five-door models were again a deliberate reflection of Discovery practice.

What McGovern didn't reveal at that first technical seminar was that the Freelander Station Wagon had ended up as too conventional in appearance for his taste. He much preferred the three-door models. But he was happy to admit to this some years later, just before he left Land Rover to join Lincoln in the USA.

The three-door models were designed with open backs. This open section could be covered either by a folding top (when the vehicle would be called the Softback) or by a resin-moulded hardtop. The softback hood was designed to fold forwards and upwards into the central rollover bar behind the front seats, and also had detachable sidescreens. Removing these allowed the vehicle to be run with open sides at the back but with the canopy roof in place.

Both five-door and three-door models had a side-hinged tail door, and Station Wagons and top-model three-doors had an ingenious electrically operated drop-glass in this. The glass could be lowered to give access to the rear by operating the remote-control 'plip'; it also lowered automatically by an inch or so whenever the rear door handle was operated. This prevented it from catching on the softback when this was in place, and reduced the chance that slamming the tail door would result in broken glass. Once the door was closed and the handle released, the glass was automatically raised into its normal 'closed' position.

Engines

As noted in Chapter Two, there were just two engines available at the Freelander's launch. At that technical seminar in July 1997, none of the engineers was prepared to discuss the well-founded rumours of a V6 at a later date. However, the V6 was in fact already on trial in prototypes by then, and the odd smile or wink in response to questions made perfectly clear that something was most definitely being planned!

The big seller was expected to be the L-series diesel. With 96bhp at 4,200rpm and 155lb ft of torque at 2,000rpm, it sounded a bit underpowered for a Land Rover – but of course, the engineers pointed out, the

Freelander was so much lighter than traditional Land Rover products that it didn't need any extra power. And in fact, they were right: although the diesel Freelander was no ball of fire, driving one for the first time did turn out to be a pleasant surprise.

In Freelander guise, it was equipped with the latest electronically controlled Bosch injection system and drive-by-wire accelerator control. That was something which was certain not to appeal to Land Rover traditionalists who were used to a direct cable connection between accelerator and diesel fuel pump, but the fact is that it worked, and worked well. Land Rover boasted that it would deliver 42mpg on the extra-urban cycle and just under 30mpg around town. In practice, an overall average of 35mpg did prove to be well within reach – a figure that was only in the fantasies of other Land Rover drivers.

As for the petrol engine, which was expected to appeal strongly but to be out-sold by the diesel, its 118bhp at 5,500rpm sounded rather more promising. It was an all-aluminium engine, with twin camshafts, four valves per cylinder and fuel injection, and for the Freelander it had been re-tuned to deliver maximum torque at lower crankshaft speeds than in its car

versions (such as the MGF). Its peak torque of 122lb ft arrived at 2,750rpm, and fuel economy was supposed to be somewhere between 21.7mpg and 32.8mpg – in other words, an overall average somewhere in the mid-20s could be expected.

It's a fact that the petrol and diesel versions of the Freelander were absolutely identical externally. It was impossible to tell one from the other, even by looking at such details as the exhaust tailpipe – so often a give-away on other vehicles which are similarly equipped with alternative diesel and petrol engines. So why were there no identifying badges? Nobody at the technical seminar was prepared to give a straight answer to that question, and the non-badging policy was not pursued on any other Land Rover product. In fact, when the next new model appeared – the Discovery Series II, which was announced in 1998 – it carried 'V8' or 'Td5' badges on the tailgate to distinguish petrol from diesel models, even though there were no badges to identify one level of trim from another.

The Freelander's engines weren't entirely new. This is the L-series diesel in a Rover 620 SLDi – where it had been introduced 1995. The car was basically a 'Roverised' Honda Accord, but the engine was a Rover design.

4x4

It was especially interesting at that technical seminar to listen to the engineers talking about the 4x4 system they had used in the Freelander. Once it had become clear that the new vehicle was to be a Land Rover, there had been no question about having all four wheels

The Freelander drivetrain laid out on the assembly line at Land Rover's Solihull assembly plant. Engine and front suspension are carried on a sub-frame which bolts to the bodyshell; the gearbox is at the front and a propshaft runs back to the viscous coupling in the centre of the vehicle.

driven. And as Land Rover was by that stage wedded to the principle of permanent four-wheel drive, it was quite clear also that all four wheels were going to have to be driven all the time.

However, that was not at all the same thing as giving the Freelander a standard Land Rover-style drivetrain with permanent four-wheel drive. That type of drivetrain is designed to give the vehicle abundant traction and plenty of low-down torque when used off the road, so that it can haul itself through or across very difficult terrain. Freelander was never intended to be that kind of vehicle. Its intended buyers were not

going to use it for heavy-duty off-road driving. They wanted its four-wheel drive to provide traction on wet grass or perhaps in snow, and above all to give better grip on ordinary tarmac roads.

So, the Freelander drivetrain was designed without a selectable low range gearset. This saved weight, saved complication, and saved costs. Nobody, except perhaps for die-hard Land Rover traditionalists, was ever going to miss those low gear ratios. At least, that's what the Freelander's designers thought. What they probably hadn't expected was that there would be a proportion of buyers who would expect the Freelander to go where

any other Land Rover could go – and who would be disappointed when it didn't.

In a normal Land Rover transmission, drive emerging from the primary gearbox is transferred to a secondary gearbox. This secondary gearbox provides two sets of gears – a high range for normal road work, and a low range for low-speed off-road work. From the 'transfer' gearbox, the drive is then taken by propshafts to differentials in the front and rear axles. In those Land

The same drivetrain is seen from the rear. Here, the rear sub-frame and its mountings are clearly visible, together with the drum brakes.

Rovers with this arrangement and permanent four-wheel drive, a third (centre) differential is fitted in the transfer gearbox between the front and rear propshaft outputs. This allows the axle shafts at one end of the vehicle to rotate at a different speed from those at the other end – as happens, for example, when the vehicle is turning a corner.

The Freelander drivetrain was much simpler. Power was taken from the Rover five-speed manual PG1 gearbox (the only one available at the vehicle's launch) to a device known as an Intermediate Reduction Drive (IRD). This replaced the familiar transfer gearbox, but only partially duplicated its functions. It geared down the output from the main gearbox by a ratio of 1.458:1, before distributing it to the front differential (actually integral with the IRD unit) and through a 90° set of bevel gears and a long propshaft to the rear differential.

How did it cope with different speeds of axle shaft rotation between front and rear? The design engineers

explained that there was a Viscous Control Unit (VCU) in the middle of the rear driveline. This unit – a fluid coupling which locks up hydraulically at a certain point to give a solid drive – allowed for those differing speeds. In fact, it was designed to allow for different speeds between the front and rear pairs of wheels at all times.

This was because the Freelander had been designed with its permanent four-wheel-drive biased towards the front pair of wheels. The idea was to give it road handling more like that of the small front-wheel drive cars with which its intended customers were likely to be familiar. So the final drive in the front differential was geared at 3.188:1 while the final drive at the rear was geared to 3.214:1. The difference between the two was completely absorbed by the VCU.

A unique and interesting feature of the IRD was that the temperature of its lubricating oil was strictly controlled through a built-in heat exchanger which used the engine coolant to draw off excess heat. That lubricant had a design life of 160,000 miles or 10 years, according to the Land Rover engineers, which meant that the IRD was unlikely to cause concern to any Freelander's first few owners.

This 'ghosted' view of a five-door Freelander was issued to the press in September 1997 and shows the overall layout of the powertrain and the strut-type suspension.

This ingenious four-wheel-drive system had been designed in conjunction with Steyr-Daimler-Puch Fahrzeugtechnik in Austria, and that company also manufactured the IRD for Land Rover. It sounded impressive at the time – though there have been several reports of Freelander rear tyres wearing out at an alarming rate, apparently when the IRD becomes faulty.

Suspension and steering

Probably all the journalists at that technical seminar had doubts about the Freelander's use of all-round independent suspension. Yes, of course it would be good on the road, because all modern cars used this type of suspension to get the best available handling and roadholding. The question-mark was over off-road performance.

It wasn't so much that all-round independent suspension broke with the Land Rover tradition of beam axles front and rear, it was more that anybody who has driven off-road knows that independent suspension can reduce a vehicle's ability to get across rough terrain. In certain circumstances, both front or both rear wheels could be pushed up into the wheelarches, thus allowing the centre of the vehicle to ground out. With beam axles, that situation is impossible: as one wheel is pushed up, so the one on the other end of the same axle is pushed down, so potentially increasing ground clearance under at least one side of the vehicle and reducing the chance of grounding out. Those journalists who had driven off-road in Japanese vehicles such as the Mitsubishi Shogun and Isuzu Trooper, which both had independent front suspension, were only too well-aware of the problem.

Nevertheless, Land Rover had clearly thought long and hard about what they were doing. Although all four of the Freelander's wheels used McPherson struts (a favourite car style of suspension because of its compactness), these struts had been designed to give unusually long wheel travel. Long wheel travel was a key feature of coil-sprung Land Rovers, allowing a wheel to drop down further than in a typical car and so to increase the chance that it would make contact with the ground in rough terrain and provide traction. That, then, was a good sign.

It came as no great surprise that the Freelander was to have power-assisted steering as standard. But what did cause a few raised eyebrows was that it was to have a rack-and-pinion system. This was car technology, and gave good, crisp handling on the road. Off the road,

however, its directness resulted in fearsome feedback at the steering wheel if one front wheel was deflected by a bump or pothole. This seemed not to be a good sign for the off-road side of the Land Rover tradition. Nevertheless, the engineers insisted that they had coped with this by mounting the steering rack high up and relying on spring deflection to provide the required compliance. As experience later showed, they were right.

Brakes

There were worrying elements in the braking system, too. Discs at the front with drums at the rear were perhaps a step backwards – every other Land Rover product of the time used disc brakes on all four wheels – but the reason for the rear drums became clear from a look at the handbrake linkage. Instead of operating on the traditional Land Rover separate drum which acted on the transmission, the handbrake acted on the rear wheels. As it is notoriously difficult to make a parking brake effective on discs, Land Rover appeared to have chosen the easy solution (well, the cheaper one, anyway) and gone for drums.

Why the concern? Because the extra mechanism and linkages required for a handbrake to operate directly on the rear wheels are prone to collecting mud and other debris and seizing solid if used on an off-road vehicle. That was why Land Rovers had traditionally had a transmission parking brake, positioned well up out of harm's way where it was unlikely to be affected by a build-up of mud. So why had Land Rover gone for a handbrake which operated on the rear wheels? The engineers explained that the Freelander's intended customers would not like the way that a transmission-braked vehicle rolls downhill an inch or so when the handbrake is applied, as the slack in the transmission is taken up. They were used to cars which stopped dead where the handbrake was applied, and that was what they were going to want from the Freelander.

It was a surprise to discover that ABS was not to be fitted as standard across the range, and that it would be an extra-cost option on entry-level models. This appeared to be purely a way of keeping the Freelander's base price down to a more attractive level, so it was a marketing decision rather than an engineering one. When fitted, ABS would come with two very interesting electronic systems which were designed to aid traction and which 'piggy-backed' on the ABS installation.

The first of these was an electronic traction control system (ETC) acting on all four wheels. Any wheel which slipped would be immediately and automatically braked, so transferring torque to its opposite number through the action of the differential between them. In tandem with the action of the inter-axle VCU which

ensured that drive would go where it was needed most, this promised to give the Freelander extremely good mobility over tricky terrain as well as sure-footed handling on a wet road.

The second new feature was called Hill Descent Control (HDC). This was actually a brilliant piece of innovation which had come out of a brainstorming session among the CB40 project team. Plumbed into the ABS system, its effect was to compensate for the lack of a low range of gears when the vehicle was descending steep slopes off the road.

The low range of gears allows an off-road vehicle to be driven very slowly – and under full control – down a steep slope where a conventional car would simply run away under the force of gravity. It multiplies the engine braking effect on the wheels, so holding the vehicle back. However, the Freelander had no low range, and the engine braking effect of its four-cylinder petrol and diesel engines was nowhere near enough to give the sort of control needed in these conditions.

HDC – operated by a yellow rocker switch just under the knob of the main gear lever – limited the downhill speed of a Freelander to 5.6mph (about walking speed) by pulsing the brakes through the ABS system. This would work only when first gear or reverse was

The interior design of the three-door models featured different upholstery and door and side trim panels from the five-door. The style and the Teal Blue colour were intended to have a more youthful appeal.

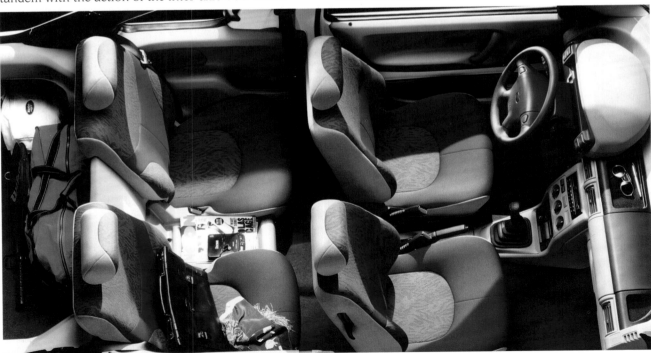

The five-doors had a very different style of upholstery and door trim panel, although the fascia was the same. Clearly visible here is the HDC control – the switch on the gear lever is identified by a yellow label.

selected and the engine was running at idling speed: a touch on the accelerator would override the system and allow the vehicle to gather speed, but backing off would again allow the HDC system to cut in and slow the Freelander down. In particularly arduous conditions, such as those where one or more wheels occasionally lost contact with the ground, the system would slow the vehicle down even further, to a governed 4.4mph, so that its driver had a better chance of keeping control.

It sounded like a brilliant idea, but of course none of the journalists was able to test it during that technical seminar at Gaydon. When they did get to test it for real a few months later, most were very impressed – although the noise it made was more than a little disconcerting.

Interior styling and appointments

To some eyes, the interior styling of the Freelander was one of its less successful aspects. What it did do was to combine the clean, uncluttered approach of the typical small car with elements of the Freelander's big brother Discovery. It even used some Discovery parts, such as the air vents and electric mirror control switch. However, the overall result was too much of a compromise, lacking the chunky ruggedness more appropriate to a Land Rover and somehow looking rather dated. Not everyone had liked the Sonar Blue trim in the early Discovery, which was repeated here with very light grey plastic trim, and those people who hadn't liked it were pretty disappointed. They were surprised, too, that the Rover stylists – some of the best in the business when it came to car interiors – had not managed to come up with something more adventurous.

Perhaps there had been a cost ceiling. Such

Some items were borrowed directly from the Discovery, such as the electric mirror 'joystick' control and the air vents.

Both three-door and five-door models had an ingenious lockable underfloor stowage box, which made use of otherwise wasted space at the rear of the vehicle. It was not very large, but it was an ideal place for concealing valuables such as cameras or handbags. However, the interior stylists had lost out to Honda here, who had incorporated the same basic idea into their CRV but had made the removable lid of the box into a folding picnic table.

Also on display at the technical seminar were several of the extra-cost accessories which were to be made available. Land Rover were already past masters at this kind of marketing, having done it very successfully when they had launched the Discovery eight years earlier. Most buyers added at least a few hundred pounds' worth of options to their basic vehicles, which of course meant bigger profits for Land Rover as well as buyers who were more satisfied that they had really personalised their vehicles.

The collection of alloy wheel options in place of the basic styled steel type was only to be expected. But some of the other options had a distinctly limited appeal, such as the add-on side mouldings which made the Freelander look as if it was wearing corrugated iron cladding ...

The launch

The next stage in the introduction of the Freelander was the first public viewing. This was planned for the Frankfurt Motor Show – probably the most important of the European shows and of course also on the German home ground of Land Rover's owners at the time, BMW.

The launch presentation to the press took place at 14.30hrs on the first press day (Tuesday, 9 September 1997) on the Rover Group stand in Hall 3. Just a week later, Land Rover followed up with the announcement that Freelanders would be the team vehicles for the 1998 Camel Trophy event, replacing the Discoverys which had done the job ever since 1990. In November, members of the world's media were invited to try the new vehicles for themselves at a ride-and-drive exercise held in the Sierra Blanca at Andalucia in Spain.

Meanwhile, in October, the Freelander took centre-stage on the Land Rover stand at the London Motor Show and generated a huge amount of interest. 'The British launch of the new Freelander attracted over 47,000 serious enquiries, well ahead of our expectations,' said a Land Rover press spokesman after the event. It looked as though everything was well on target for a major success.

considerations had certainly dictated that a passenger's side airbag would cost extra on entry-level models, although it would be standard on the top-of-the-range types. As required by law in most countries by this stage, a driver's airbag was to be standard on all models.

There were to be some important interior differences between three-door and five-door models. Most obvious was that the five-doors would have a 60–40 split-fold rear bench seat, while the three-doors would have two individual rear seats with a central 'console' tray between them – although a 60–40 split-fold bench would be optional. The upholstery was also to differ between the two models. Both were to be finished in two complementary styles of printed fabric, but three-doors had Jungle and Trek fabric while five-doors had Tapestry and Canvas. Their very names said a lot about the differences between them – the three-door fabrics were louder and the five-door types more sober, although certainly not conventional – and these differences were reinforced by differently shaped panels. Those on the three-doors were more dramatic and swoopy than the relatively restrained five-door types, but both were clearly from the same school of thought.

Chapter **Four**

The first three years

1.8 petrol and 2.0 diesel, 1998–2000

Freelanders started reaching the buying public through UK showrooms during January 1998, although of course, several hundred early examples had been registered as demonstration and development vehicles by Land Rover before that date. Sales in some other territories also began in January, and the Freelander was gradually rolled out to all the countries on its initial 'hit-list' over the next few months. The Australian launch, for example, was in February, while the French debut took place in April.

Right from the start, the Freelander was a sales success. Bargain-basement prices in the first few months helped, and Freelanders went on sale in the UK with a starting-price of £15,995. Whether by coincidence or not, that had also been the starting-price of the Land Rover Discovery when it had been introduced in 1989.

Of course, few people paid just £15,995 for one of

Representative of the volume-production Freelander Station Wagons is this one. The door window surrounds are now finished in the body colour – compare with the early model on page 54.

THE 1.8-LITRE K-SERIES PETROL ENGINE

The Freelander's 1.8-litre four-cylinder engine is a member of the K-series family drawn up by the Rover Group in the late 1980s. The engines were designed from the outset for transverse installation, and were the long-overdue replacements for the old A-series engine which dated right back to 1952.

The K-series was an ultra-modern design, with a belt-driven camshaft and all-alloy construction. It was constructed from a series of horizontal 'layers' clamped together by long bolts running from top to bottom of the engine. These bolts served as both cylinder head bolts and main bearing studs, as well as contributing to the engine's overall rigidity and allowing better stress and expansion control. Lean-burn technology combined with a catalytic converter to give clean running, while hydraulic tappets reduced noise and servicing requirements.

The K-series was also designed to allow for variations in both swept volume and cylinder head design. The first versions (introduced in October 1989 for the Rover 200 Series) had a 1.4-litre capacity with a single overhead camshaft and two valves per cylinder. However, later on came 1.1-litre, 1.6-litre and 1.8-litre versions, some of them with twin overhead camshafts and four valves per cylinder. The 1.6-litre and 1.8-litre 'Big K' versions of the engine also had a special stepped cylinder liner.

The 1.8-litre engine entered production in 1995 for the MGF sports car, and was the version chosen as the basis of the Freelander's engine. For the Freelander, it was modified in several ways. Re-tuning of the injection and intake systems brought the torque peak down to 2,750rpm from the 3,000rpm of the sports car, while the intake duct mouldings were waterproofed and the ignition coil mounted higher up to make the engine more suitable for off-road use.

During the 1998, 1999 and 2000 model-years, this engine was rated at 120bhp with 121lb ft of torque in the Freelander, and was simply known as the 1.8. Later, modified examples were known as 1.8i types.

The 1.8-litre K-series petrol engine looked somewhat lost in an engine bay designed to receive the much bigger 2.5-litre V6. However, mounting the engine low down did keep the vehicle's centre of gravity low, too. This example was pictured in a prototype Freelander that was displayed at the press briefing in July 1997.

these early Freelanders. That price tag applied only to the entry-level three-door softback with the 1.8-litre petrol engine. Every other model was more expensive – up to £20,995 for the diesel five-door Station Wagon – and Land Rover dealers had been well-briefed to promote sales of add-on accessories which bumped up the showroom price.

There was a clear hierarchy within the Freelander range right from the start. Softback three-doors were always cheaper than hardback versions, and these in turn were always cheaper than the five-door Station Wagons. Diesel-engined Freelanders always cost more than the equivalent petrol-engined models, and there

were two specification levels in the UK (although other markets had a model mix and specifications to suit local conditions). However, none of these Freelanders ever carried model identification badges; not only was it impossible to distinguish petrol from diesel models (see Chapter Three) but it was also impossible to tell entry-level specification from top-level specification without a close look at the vehicle.

These first Freelanders were available for three model-years (1998, 1999 and 2000), and were actually on sale for about 21 months. They were the vehicles which firmly established the Freelander as yet another success story for Land Rover – and what a success it was!

THE 2.0-LITRE L-SERIES DIESEL ENGINE

Like the original Land Rover petrol engine back in 1948, the diesel engine used in the first Freelanders was designed primarily for saloon cars.

Known to its manufacturers in the Rover Group as the L-series, the engine had been specifically intended for transverse installation to go with the front-wheel-drive configurations used in Rover cars. It was a four-cylinder turbocharged direct-injection type with a 2-litre (1,994cc) capacity and electronic control, and had entered production in 1994, making its first appearance in the 600 Series cars the following January. Both car and Freelander versions of the L-series engine were built at Land Rover's Solihull site.

Design work had started on the L-series diesel in mid-1992, and the engine was developed by a 'corporate' diesel engineering team drawn from both Rover Cars and Land Rover, together with input from several petrol unit engineers. It drew on existing Rover design and manufacturing experience — notably sharing its 84.5mm bore and 88.9mm stroke with the Rover MDi and T-series petrol engines — but was a genuinely new unit, initially incorporating 241 completely new components. Its all-new cylinder block was made of cast iron and featured siamesed bores for compactness. The aluminium cylinder head had two vertical valves per cylinder, driven via hydraulic tappets from a belt-driven single overhead camshaft, and the turbocharger was a Garrett GT15 type with variable wastegate control and an intercooler.

Team working techniques (as pioneered in the late 1980s by the team which drew up the Land Rover Discovery) allowed the first prototype engine to be running by August 1992, and the L-series went from concept to production in a remarkably short period of two and a half years. It was notably cost-efficient by world industry standards of the time: of the £30 million it cost to bring to production, £16 million was for manufacturing facilities for the initial production phase.

The L-series diesel had Bosch two-stage fuel injection and a single overhead camshaft driven by toothed belt. In Freelander form, it had undergone some 40 modifications from its original saloon car form, and these included a relocated turbocharger (and consequently a special manifold design), a bigger starter motor and alternator, and an oil cooler.

As tuned to suit the Freelander, the engine had 94bhp at 4,200rpm and 154lb ft of torque at 2,000rpm. Car versions (in the Rover 620 models) had 105PS (103.6bhp) at the same 4,200rpm and a very similar 155lb ft at 2,000rpm, and an 86PS (84.9bhp) version was made available in the Rover 220D and 220SD from October 1995. It was a frugal and flexible engine, although in the Freelander it could never be described as either exciting or vigorous!

DID YOU KNOW?
Ladies off the road

Two days after the Freelander's launch in France, Rover France announced that it was entering one of the new vehicles in an adventure rally-raid. This event was known as the Trophée des Gazelles (the Gazelle Trophy) and was open only to all-female teams.

The Freelander was co-sponsored by *Madame Figaro* magazine, whose journalist Valérie Bailly joined Rover France's Marie-Laure Coissac to form the crew.

A Freelander was entered in the all-woman Trophée des Gazelles in 1998.

The sales story

Within a few weeks of the vehicle going on sale to the public, Land Rover knew that they had got the Freelander right. The careful market research, vehicle development, and pre-launch marketing campaign had all been right on target.

'The recently launched Freelander is a resounding success and will almost double our UK sales volume in 1998,' said a delighted Peter Kinnaird, Land Rover UK's commercial director, in February that year. That doubling of sales volumes was not achieved without additional expenditure, however, and during 1998 Land

DID YOU KNOW?
Press and demo cars

At around the time of the vehicle's launch, Land Rover registered a large number of Freelanders for press and demonstration purposes. Many of these were from the first 1,500 vehicles to be built (and so Station Wagons had the blacked-out side window frames). In Britain, these vehicles were mainly registered in the R... BAC sequence.

An early curiosity

The original plan was for five-door Freelanders to have their door window frames painted black. This idea came from stylist Gerry McGovern, who saw it as a way of increasing the Freelander's family likeness to the Discovery and Range Rover.

However, there were problems on production. David Roots, a member of the Freelander project team, remembered that, 'We were repairing a lot of door frames, and incurring mismatches front to rear, forcing another repair (all very costly)... The repair work was also considered to be too time-consuming and would pose a large problem due to the amount of vehicles to be produced.'

The first Freelander Station Wagons had blacked-out frames around the door windows, but this was changed early on because it caused problems in production.

So the blacked-out frames were abandoned at VIN 501925, after about 1,500 vehicles had been produced. 'The change further negated a process in the paint shop,' said Roots, 'saving further money, and all round it was felt that it would be cheaper to produce colour-coded window frames . . . It was also felt that coloured frames suited the vehicle better.'

TEETHING TROUBLES

Like most new cars, the Freelander suffered from some build faults in its first few months. As these faults came to light, so assembly line procedures were altered to eliminate them.

The most serious early faults were steering column locks which were stiff or jammed, a whistle from the central control unit behind the fuse box, and loose PAS hoses (except on RHD diesel models). These were rectified by dealers under warranty. However, there were many other teething troubles in the Freelander's early days.

All models could suffer from wind whistle at speed from gaps between the front bumper and the headlights and wings, and from a squeak from the bonnet hinge as the bonnet was opened. Heater blowers could whistle and vibrate – the latter quite badly on some vehicles – and the rear side windows could mist up because of a blocked vent. Air-conditioned models could suffer from generally poor demisting. The front seat slides were often insufficiently lubricated on assembly, while the rear seat squabs could be difficult to latch and unlatch.

On Station Wagons, the driver's seat could be affected by a squeak from its lumbar adjustment cable, while the rear seat's release cable could become trapped and its centre armrest bracket could squeak. On diesel engines, there were leaks from the oil filter, while there were oil leaks from the camshaft cover of petrol engines.

Customers also complained about some of the unfamiliar characteristics of the Freelander, and Land Rover dealers were instructed to explain patiently to them that these were not faults. Among these characteristics were noise from the ABS modulator on start-up (a warning about this was added to the third and later editions of the Owners' Handbook) and a slight braking effect at low speed when on full lock (a normal effect of the viscous coupling in the driveline). Customers who complained that their headlamps misted up internally were also told that this was 'normal' – which cannot have been very reassuring!

Rover dealers in the UK invested some £122 million of their own money redeveloping existing premises and building new ones to accommodate the expansion.

UK sales were probably helped by the announcement of a three-year dealer warranty in April 1998, Land Rover's earlier and less-generous warranty having lagged somewhat behind that offered by other manufacturers. The warranty placed no limitations on mileage or on the items covered during the first year, while the second and third years gave cover up to 60,000 miles.

This and other marketing initiatives, coupled to the

Freelander's real appeal to its target audience, allowed sales to take off with a rush. In the first quarter of 1998, the model took a 23 per cent share of the light 4x4 market in the UK. Sales continued to increase; for the first quarter of 1999, it was 28 per cent and by the end of April 1999, the new Land Rover occupied the top slot in the UK 4x4 sales charts, having sold more than twice as many as its nearest competitor. Gratifyingly for Solihull, the second best-seller in the UK was its own Discovery Series II!

The Freelander's success was certainly not confined to the domestic market, however. That spring, Land

Rover was able to claim that it had become the best-selling 4x4 off-road vehicle in Europe, outselling its nearest rival by more than 40 per cent.

Equipment levels

The two specification levels in the UK could be seen simply as entry-level and high-line; entry-level models were known as Freelander i types (or di types if diesel-powered), while the high-line models were called Freelander XEi (or XEdi) types. There were some quite important differences in the specification of each of these models.

All entry-level Freelanders came with a driver's side airbag, remote-control central locking, electric front windows and electrically adjustable heated door mirrors, and 15-inch styled steel wheels on 195/80 R 15 tyres. The ICE system was a Philips-made R660 stereo radio-cassette FM-MW-LW head unit with a detachable keypad. Power-assisted steering was standard, and of course a five-speed manual gearbox was the only option with both petrol and diesel engines.

Softback three-doors of course had the softback itself with a PVC tail door window, individual rear seats with a centre console tray and twin opaque targa roof panels. Hardback three-doors came with the detachable hardback, electrically operated tail door glass with a heating element and wash-wipe, and hinged rear quarter windows. Entry-level five-doors had a 60–40 split rear bench seat, adjustable lumbar support for the driver's seat, and rear grab handles.

The high-line XEi and XEdi models were much better equipped. This specification brought ABS, Electronic Traction Control (ETC) and Hill Descent Control (HDC) on all models, plus a passenger's side airbag, and 15-inch five-spoke alloy wheels with locking wheel nuts.

The XEi and XEdi Softbacks had a glass tail door window in place of the PVC type on base models, and both these and the Hardbacks had glass targa roof panels instead of the opaque type, a tail door stowage

A Freelander XEi or XEdi Softback model shows the open back which was expected to have such strong sales appeal.

net, and an uprated ICE system. This consisted of an R770 head unit, colour-keyed to the fascia, with similar features to the R660 in cheaper models but with the addition of RDS, CD compatibility and a remote display facility mounted centrally below the windscreen. This display showed all the relevant clock, radio-cassette and RDS information. There were six speakers, the additional two being mounted in the front door mirror cheater panels. The XEi and XEdi five-doors also had the six-speaker ICE and tail door stowage net, plus a retractable loadspace cover and an electric spoiler-style glass sunroof.

Options

Land Rover had learned the value of a wide range of accessories from its sales of the Discovery. From the customer's point of view, these allowed individual buyers to 'personalise' their vehicles – an important attraction in an age of the mass production of essentially identical items. From the dealer's point of view, their benefit was in increasing the point-of-sale cost and therefore the profit; the typical buyer of a £16,000 Freelander might spend a further £1,000 on accessories which made the vehicle suit his or her lifestyle better.

For the Freelander, Land Rover had decided that the very nature of the vehicle and its entirely new market

DID YOU KNOW?
Conquest sales

Land Rover focused its initial Freelander marketing efforts on 'conquest' sales – selling to buyers who were not already owners of a Land Rover product and who were not owners of competitive 4x4s either.

Only around 15 per cent of sales were expected to be to owners of competitive compact 4x4s. The largest target market (of 27 per cent) was expected to be existing owners of cars in the upper medium sector. Next in line were lower medium car owners (16 per cent) and small car owners (7 per cent). Lesser percentages were expected from other sectors such as MPVs and Executive cars, while around 10 per cent of Freelander sales world-wide were expected to go to those who were buying one as an addition to an existing fleet and not as a replacement vehicle.

DID YOU KNOW?
Freelander 'Number 1'

The first production Freelander did not carry serial number 1. In fact, its serial number was 677 (SALLNABA7WA-600677 to be exact). Although off-tools Freelander production had started at 600001, the first 676 vehicles to be built were pre-production prototypes used for assembly trials, development testing, and all the other start-up work associated with the introduction of a brand-new model.

The first production Freelander was a five-door Station Wagon with the 1.8-litre petrol engine, right-hand drive and the standard five-speed manual gearbox. It was painted in Chawton White and its bodywork was signed in felt pen by all those who had been involved in its build, and by the principal designers and engineers involved with the CB40 project.

Production Freelander Number 1 was signed by all those involved in its design and construction.

The vehicle was then handed over to the Heritage Motor Centre at Gaydon for its museum collection. Unfortunately, the signatures were not first protected by a coat of clear varnish. This meant that the vehicle could not be taken outside in case of rain, and also made it vulnerable to graffiti and vandalism from museum visitors.

Several earlier Freelanders still survived at the time of writing. The earliest one known was 600007 (the seventh off-tools example), an unregistered and unbadged five-door Station Wagon which was on loan to the famous Dunsfold Collection of Land Rovers based at Dunsfold in Surrey.

Three Fifty-50 vehicles on display. The very early three-door model on the right was used as a publicity vehicle for the event.

THE FIFTY-50 CHALLENGE

The Fifty-50 Challenge was a charity fund-raising event held during Land Rover's 50th Anniversary year and featuring Freelanders. A team of volunteers from among Land Rover and Rover employees (the two companies were then both owned by BMW) drove the three vehicles through 50 countries in 50 days of their own time, and sponsorship arranged in advance enabled them to collect their target of £400,000 (or more?) for the motor industry charity, BEN.

Three early production Freelanders (with blacked-out door window frames) were used for the Fifty-50 Challenge. The back-up vehicle, based on a military-pattern Defender 'Wolf', was affectionately known as 'Goldilocks'.

The total distance covered was 20,000 miles; the vehicles set out at the beginning of August and finished their trip in mid-September.

The three Freelanders were all early production five-door models, painted in a striking light blue and gold livery and carrying sponsors' logos. They were registered as R258 CDU, R262 CDU and R280 CDU. Two of these vehicles still survive, one in the Heritage Motor Centre at Gaydon and the other in the Dunsfold Collection in Surrey.

The vehicles were accompanied by a specially prepared Defender 110 support vehicle. Painted in all-over gold, this vehicle was nicknamed 'Goldilocks' and is today also cared for by the Dunsfold Collection.

There was in fact also a fourth Freelander painted in the Fifty-50 livery and used for promotional purposes. This was a three-door pre-production example, registered as K311 KWT.

DID YOU KNOW?

The *Tomb Raider* Freelander that wasn't

When film director Simon West decided to make a movie version of the hugely popular *Tomb Raider* interactive computer game, he also decided to indulge his passion for Land Rovers. In the computer game, heroine Lara Croft does not drive a Land Rover — but in the West movie, released in mid-2001 as *Lara Croft: Tomb Raider*, she was seen behind the wheel of a specially-prepared Land Rover Defender 110 High-Capacity Pick-Up.

When West approached Land Rover with his initial idea, the company's Special Vehicles division (which creates bespoke vehicles for the utility and luxury markets) was tasked with delivering what he wanted. Not wanting to miss an opportunity,

The Freelander *Tomb Raider* prototype was unfortunately not used in the movie. It is seen here while on display at the Land Rover Gear Shop in the Xscape Centre at Milton Keynes.

Land Rover Special Vehicles created not only a *Tomb Raider* Defender (three visually identical ones, in fact, to meet the requirements of filming in several different locations) but also a *Tomb Raider* Freelander.

Sadly, the Freelander didn't make the final cut of the movie, but the specially-equipped three-door model did get seen in public — when it was displayed in late 2001 at the Land Rover Gear Shop in Milton Keynes' Xscape Centre. Land Rover later made a *Tomb Raider* limited edition Defender, but there was no equivalent for the Freelander — except in Hungary, as the sidebar in Chapter Five explains.

The *Tomb Raider* vehicle had a special dashboard, in black, which would later become a feature of production models. Note the simple twist-start switch – Lara Croft wouldn't have had time for things like keys . . .

Some elements tried out on the *Tomb Raider* Freelander were designed to give it a tough image, although they might not have been all that practical in the real world.

sector justified a radical new approach. So, instead of the 50 or so accessories which might have been expected, more than 100 items were listed in the Freelander accessory catalogue by the time the vehicle went on sale.

The Millennium Edition, or Freelander MM, featured the latest Alveston Red paint with a number of otherwise optional accessories as standard.

Many items on the accessory list were of course directly sourced from factory-fit components, such as the interchangeable hardback and softback, and the roof racks. There were add-ons, too, such as the six-disc CD autochanger which could be specified (at extra cost) with the R770 ICE system and which was fitted under the front passenger seat.

However, the main range of accessories offered customers the ability to personalise their Freelanders in many different ways. Exterior appearance items included auxiliary driving lamps, polymer nudge bars, body styling mouldings, alloy wheels, chip-resistant graphic body tapes, and side steps. Amenity accessories allowed the vehicle to be tailored to different user patterns. For the loadspace alone, there was a range of liners, dog guards, stowage nets and security covers. For three-door models there was a quick-fit shower cover to suit a change in the weather if the hardback or softback had been left at home, and there were also practical seat covers. One of the 'flagship' accessories for the three-door was a rear seat centre console box, which fitted between the two individual rear seats and served as an armrest, map holder, cup holder and portable picnic box all rolled into one.

Lifestyle accessories encompassed roof boxes, bicycle and ski racks, and a variety of different tow bars and emergency equipment. Electrical equipment such as a cool box could be plugged into the power socket in the rear of the centre console, while there was an additional accessory-fit socket for the loadspace.

Range adjustments

The original two-level specification line-up lasted for less than three months in the UK. Feedback from customers and scrutiny of the options which were being taken up showed Land Rover that there was a need for a third

THE FREELANDER COMMERCIAL

In April 1999, at the Fleet Motor Show held at the Birmingham NEC, Land Rover announced a van derivative of the three-door hardback Freelander, known as the Commercial. Deliveries to customers began in September, thus making the first production Freelander Commercials 2000 model-year variants.

The Freelander Commercial was available with either the 1.8-litre petrol engine or the 2.0-litre diesel, and was completed by Land Rover's Special Vehicles division at Solihull from part-finished three-door vehicles assembled on the main production lines. The unique feature of its body was a version of the resin hardback without side windows. This was normally finished in the same grey as on passenger models, but could also be supplied painted to match the bodywork. Base models lacked ABS with ETC and HDC, although these features could be supplied at extra cost.

The van body behind the seats had a capacity of 1,400 litres (50 cubic feet) and the Freelander had a payload of 580kg (1,280lb). Unique interior trim panels incorporated lashing points, a three-quarters mesh bulkhead and heavy-duty floor covering. Interior options included a checker plate floor and shelving and racking systems.

The Freelander Commercial could also be fitted with a roof rack and stowage for ladders and pipes, while various roof-mounted beacons and light bars were also available. In addition, the full range of options for the standard three-door Freelander could be ordered.

Land Rover hoped to sell the vehicle to major fleets, small businesses and people who need to transport equipment to remote off-road areas. Customers were expected to include utility, plant hire and construction companies, as well as those who wanted a stylish alternative to a conventional van or estate car.

Solihull also anticipated finding customers among the emergency services, particularly police, fire and mountain rescue teams. In the UK, however, only one Freelander Commercial is known to have been sold to a police force before the introduction of the revised 2001 models. This was a diesel model bought by the Staffordshire Police in July 2000 and registered as X179 XBF. It was allocated to the Collision Investigation Unit of the Traffic Department.

The Commercial was a neat and stylish van variant of the three-door Hardback.

The 50th Anniversary models also showcased the new leather upholstery which became an option for the 1999 model-year.

VIN CODES FOR FREELANDERS (1998–2000)

The VIN codes used in this period consisted of 17 characters, made up of an 11-character prefix code and a six-digit serial number.

Example: SALLNAAA7WA-123456.

This breaks down as follows:

SAL   Manufacturer code (Rover Group)

LN   Freelander

A   Standard trim

    B = Commercial trim

A   Three-door body (Hardback or Softback)

    B = Five-door body (Station Wagon)

A   1.8-litre K-series petrol engine (HOU spec)

    B = 2.0-litre L-series diesel engine

    C = 1.8-litre K-series petrol engine (LOU spec)

    D = 1.8-litre K-series petrol engine (LOL spec)

    F = 1.8-litre K-series petrol engine (HOL spec)

7   RHD with 5-speed manual gearbox

    8 = LHD with 5-speed manual gearbox

W   Model-year 1998

    X = 1999 Y = 2000

A   Assembled at Solihull

123456 Serial number

specification level which fitted between the two early ones. From mid-March 1998, the five-door range was broadened by Xi and Xdi variants, which were aimed at the corporate and fleet sales market. These models came with 15-inch alloy wheels, air conditioning, metallic paint and the loadspace cover as standard.

Next on the agenda were changes for the 1999 model-year, which began in the late summer of 1998. However, there were no major changes; two of the exterior colours were changed, in line with similar changes for other Land Rover products at the same time. Otherwise, the 1999 Freelanders remained the same as the 1998 models, and (registration dates apart), the only easy way of distinguishing one from another is by the model-year identifier in the VIN code. As the accompanying sidebar shows, if this is a 'W', the vehicle is a 1998 model, while an 'X' indicates a 1999 model.

Nevertheless, the 1999 model-year was given a kick-start by the limited-edition 50th Anniversary Freelanders (see page 63). These were the first Freelanders to be offered with leather upholstery, all standard production models of the time having fabric seat coverings.

There were further changes, again prompted by customer feedback, for the 2000 model-year Freelanders which went on sale in August 1999. All entry-level (i and di) models were fitted with the six-speaker ICE system with RDS, while entry-level three-doors gained glass targa roof panels and five-doors came with the loadspace cover as standard. The mid-range Xi and Xdi five-doors were now viewed as the core models in the range, and were joined by Xi and Xdi three-door Softbacks and Hardbacks. All these mid-range models came with 15-inch alloy wheels, the six-speaker ICE with RDS, ABS, ETC and HDC.

At the top of the range, the XEi and XEdi came with air conditioning, 16-inch sports alloy wheels and mud-flaps, while roof rails were standard on five-door derivatives. Leather upholstery – previewed on the previous year's 50th Anniversary Collector's Edition in the UK – was now standard, with combination Light and Dark Smokestone seat facings and an ash leather steering wheel rim cover. Three-door XEi and XEdi derivatives, which were delayed until October 1999, had seat facings in Light Smokestone and Teal leather and had three-seater rear bench seats in place of the twin rear seats of lower-priced models. The 2000 model-year also brought seven new exterior colours while the Freelander range was broadened by the addition of a Commercial variant (see pages 61 and 64).

THE FREELANDER 50th ANNIVERSARY EDITION

The year 1998 marked the 50th anniversary of the Land Rover marque, the first Land Rover utility having gone on sale in the spring of 1948 after being displayed at the Amsterdam Motor Show in April.

Special 50th Anniversary collector's editions of the Range Rover, Discovery and Defender went on sale in June 1998, but the Freelander equivalent was held over until September. Three different models were available, based on the five-door Station Wagon, the three-door Softback and the three-door Hardback. Station Wagons and Hardbacks could be had with either the petrol or the diesel engine, but Softbacks came only with the petrol engine.

There were just 3,000 of these Freelanders in total. They were available in Atlantis Blue, the special colour reserved for all Land Rover's 50th Anniversary limited editions, and probably most of them had this. However, the Softback and Hardback variants were also supplied in Blenheim Silver — one of the colours new for the 1999 model-year — while the Station Wagons could be ordered in White Gold. All models came with two-tone leather upholstery.

The Station Wagons were based on the top-specification XEi or XEdi models, and all came with 16-inch alloy wheels, roof rails, aluminium side steps, air conditioning and a CD autochanger. Hardbacks also had 16-inch alloy wheels, air conditioning, ABS with

The 50th Anniversary special edition three-door is seen here with its Softback rolled up. Note the add-on side mouldings, the rear roof bars, the side runners and the light guards which were standard on this model. Atlantis Blue was unique to the 50th Anniversary Collector's Edition Land Rovers.

ETC and HDC, and were provided with an accessory cool-hot box in the boot. Softbacks, however, were distinguished by a body styling kit, 17-inch sport alloy wheels, rear roof bars, glass targa roof panels, spot and fog lights, a soft nudge bar and stainless steel protection rails, while their interiors featured a CD autochanger and rigid loadspace cover.

Always more sober than the three-door, the Station Wagon was still distinctive in 50th Anniversary form.

COLOURS AND TRIMS

1998 model-year (January to August 1998)

The same 10 paint finishes were available for both three-door and five-door Freelanders. There were three solid colours, four metallic finishes and three micatallics.

Three-doors could be bought with a choice of Teal (blue) or Smokestone (grey) trim; in each case the upholstery was made up of two different fabrics, one called Jungle and one called Trek. Five-doors always had grey trim with upholstery in two different fabrics called Tapestry and Canvas.

The paint colours were:
Altai Silver (metallic)
Beluga Black (solid)
Caledonian Blue (solid)
Charleston Green (metallic)
Chawton White (solid)
Cobar Blue (metallic)
Epsom Green (micatallic)
Rioja Red (micatallic)
Venetian Mauve (micatallic)
White Gold (metallic)

1999 model-year (September 1998 to August 1999)

The 10 paint finishes available for the 1999 model-year were changed only slightly from the 1998 range. Blenheim Silver replaced Altai Silver (both metallics), and Java Black (micatallic) replaced Beluga Black (solid). This left a range of two solid colours, four metallic finishes and four micatallics.

Interior trim options were unchanged from the 1998 range. The paint colours were:
Blenheim Silver (metallic)
Caledonian Blue (solid)
Charleston Green (metallic)
Chawton White (solid)
Cobar Blue (metallic)
Epsom Green (micatallic)
Java Black (micatallic)
Rioja Red (micatallic)
Venetian Mauve (micatallic)
White Gold (metallic)

Note that Atlantis Blue (metallic) was also available on the 1999-model 50th Anniversary Collector's Edition only.

2000 model-year (October 1999 to August 2000)

A range of 13 paint finishes was offered for the 2000 model-year. New colours Alveston Red, Appalachian Green, Icelandic Blue, Kent Green, Kinversand Bronze, Oxford Blue and Rutland Red replaced Caledonian Blue, Charleston Green, Rioja Red and Venetian Mauve. There were again two solid colours, while the metallics were reduced in number to three and the remaining eight were micatallics.

Interior trim was rationalised. Three-door models still had a choice of Teal or Smokestone upholstery, although the fabric was now simply called Jungle. Five-doors came with a choice of Smokestone or Dark Smokestone Tapestry fabrics. Certain combinations of interior and exterior colours were 'recommended' (i.e. standard) although the alternative interior colour was always available to special order. Leather upholstery was made available, and on three-doors combined panels of Teal and Smokestone colours, while on five-doors it combined Light and Dark Smokestone.

The 'recommended' combinations were as follows:

Alveston Red (micatallic)	Smokestone (all models)
Appalachian Green (micatallic)	Smokestone (3-dr) or Dark Smokestone (5-dr)
Blenheim Silver (metallic)	Smokestone (3-dr) or Dark Smokestone (5-dr)
Chawton White (solid)	Teal (3-dr) or Dark Smokestone (5-dr)
Cobar Blue (metallic)	Teal (3-dr) or Smokestone (5-dr)
Epsom Green (micatallic)	Smokestone (all models)
Icelandic Blue (micatallic)	Teal (3-dr) or Smokestone (5-dr)
Java Black (micatallic)	Teal (3-dr) or Dark Smokestone (5-dr)
Kent Green (micatallic)	Smokestone (3-dr) or Dark Smokestone (5-dr)
Kinversand Bronze (micatallic)	Smokestone (3-dr) or Dark Smokestone (5-dr)
Oxford Blue (micatallic)	Smokestone (all models)
Rutland Red (solid)	Smokestone (all models)
White Gold (metallic)	Smokestone (all models)

FREELANDER AND THE UK POLICE, 1998–2000

Land Rover has traditionally sold its products in quite large quantities to UK police forces, and at the time of the Freelander's launch many traffic divisions were using Range Rovers or Discoverys for motorway patrol duties while Defenders featured in some fleets for special duties, such as towing mobile command centres. So it was only to be expected that the company would attempt to interest police buyers in its new model.

The five-door Station Wagon was always going to be more suited for police work than the three-door models because the extra doors afforded greater accessibility to the area behind the crew seats at the front. The first police concept vehicle appears to have been R909 BDU, which was displayed at events in the summer of 1998 associated with Land Rover's 50th Anniversary celebrations. However, this was probably not the first demonstrator proper. That appears to have been T428 JOP, which was not registered until May 1999.

T428 JOP was a diesel model, but the next two police demonstrator Freelanders (V184 LOB and V962 LOB, both registered in January 2000) had the 1.8-litre petrol engine. As most UK police forces depended on diesel engines by this time, it seems probable that those who tried the initial diesel demonstrator found it too slow, and so Solihull tried a different tactic in order to attract orders.

One other problem which deterred Police sales was that the Freelander did not offer a large internal load area. It was too small (and far too slow) to be suitable for traffic patrol duties, but it did have appeal for niche duties in traffic divisions, in the roles of accident or crash investigation units. There were also some areas where the vehicle was well suited to use by rural Police patrols.

The first Freelanders to enter police service in the UK were a pair of diesel-engined models bought by the Royal Ulster Constabulary and registered in March 1999. Just a few days later, the Cambridgeshire Constabulary took the first of three petrol-engined models into service.

Thereafter, Freelanders entered service with the Sussex Police, Wiltshire Constabulary, Leicestershire Constabulary, Avon and Somerset Constabulary, South Yorkshire Police, Northern Constabulary and Staffordshire Police. In all, a total of between 20 and 25 Freelanders entered police service during the first three years of the vehicle's production.

Not every UK police force which took these early Freelanders was very impressed. There were some repeat orders, but some forces experienced reliability problems and turned to other 4x4s as replacements. In general, the 2001 and later models with their more powerful engines were a bigger hit with police users in the UK.

(I am indebted to police vehicle expert Peter Hall for much of the above information.)

Freelander Station Wagons found favour with some police forces in the UK. Andy Bardsley's picture shows the first example to enter service with a Scottish force – the Northern Constabularly.

Chapter Five

Major makeover

The 2001 model-year Freelanders

Even though the Freelander had proved an enormous success right from the start, Land Rover could not afford to rest on its laurels. While the money was coming in from sales of the first models, a good proportion of the profits was being spent on improvements which would allow the model to retain its appeal in the face of new rivals.

This development was of course envisaged right from the start. The Freelander was targeted at fashion-conscious buyers, and so it could not be allowed to become unfashionable. In consequence, a development programme to keep it fresh had been started almost as soon as the initial production specification had been signed off in 1996.

The Freelander was scheduled to go on sale at the start of 1998, and the plan was that it should be replaced by a new model some time around 2005, a six-to-seven-year lifespan being as much as Land Rover felt able to risk. The requirement to please a very fashion-conscious market persuaded the company to decide on a strategy involving two upgrades during that lifespan.

DID YOU KNOW?

In charge

As noted in Chapter Two, the original project director for the Freelander was Dick Elsy, who was promoted to a more senior position within the Rover Group in 1998. The vacancy at the head of the Freelander project was filled by Elsy's Number Two, Steve Haywood, who took charge of the changes needed for the 2001 models. Once those had been successfully launched in Autumn 2000, Haywood moved on to take charge of model-year upgrades for the Discovery Series II and to run the project (L319) for its replacement. He was succeeded by Keith Newman.

The first upgrade would be made after the vehicle had been on sale for between two and three years, and would provide a shot in the arm from improvements which the customers would see as exciting and which would also make the Freelander attractive to a wider customer base. Then, the second upgrade would be a more cosmetic facelift around three years later – details of which were announced shortly before this book went to press.

Plans were made in mid-2000 to introduce the first round of improvements – the ones which would broaden the Freelander's appeal for the 2001 model-year. This gave a development time of around four years from the point where the specification of the first models had been frozen, and would allow around two years (from 1998) for more minor modifications inspired by customer feedback to be incorporated.

The area for major modifications was immediately identified as that of the drivetrain – in other words, the engine and transmissions. While the Rover K-series petrol engine and L-series diesel both delivered good performance, there was no doubt that Freelander customers would soon be asking for more – or that rival vehicles due for release in the late 1990s would offer better performance to tempt customers away from the Freelander. Similarly, while there was nothing inherently wrong with the Rover PG1 five-speed manual gearbox which would go into the first production models, there was no automatic-transmission alternative. It would not be long before customers made clear that they wanted such a version, and the provision of an automatic gearbox would assist Land Rover's plans to move the Freelander subtly up-market.

When work started on the 2001-model Freelanders, Land Rover was wholly owned by BMW, and so it was no surprise to find their engineers turning to BMW componentry for some of these improvements. However, at this stage the company still enjoyed a very close relationship with Rover Cars, which was also owned by BMW, and so the engineers also took a close look at the latest Rover drivetrain hardware.

The BMW diesel

BMW was justly famous for the excellence of its engines, but perhaps the most exciting of its recent developments had been in the field of diesel power units. The company had put its first diesel into production as long ago as 1983, and that 2,443cc turbocharged straight-six engine had immediately gained acclaim as the most refined engine of its type anywhere in the world. It was powerful, torquey and frugal, too, and achieved the same standards of reliability and durability as the renowned BMW petrol engines of the time.

So it had been no great surprise that Land Rover had turned to BMW when its engineers were looking for a powerful and refined diesel engine to use in the second-generation Range Rover, which was under development in the early 1990s. At that stage, the German company was just about to introduce an improved six-cylinder engine of 2,498 cc, which actually became available in its 525 tds models in 1991. A deal was done for BMW to supply a version of this engine for the Range Rover when production of the new model began in 1994. By the time production started, BMW had in fact bought the Rover Group and Land Rover with it – but the diesel-engine deal was signed long before the German company had shown any interest in buying the British one, despite what some eager, but misinformed members of the media suggested at the time.

Of course, engine development did not stand still in Germany. For their third-generation diesels, the BMW engineers planned some important advances. In place of the indirect injection system used in their earlier

The big news for 2001 was the two new engines. This underbonnet view shows the BMW-built Td4 diesel, which proved by far the more popular. As was usual by this stage, the engine itself was concealed beneath cosmetic plastic covers.

diesel engines, they chose the more fuel-efficient direct injection, confident that they would be able to reduce this system's inherently greater noise levels by using a two-stage injection system. This provided a pilot injection of fuel to begin the combustion process before the main charge was delivered.

SPECIFICATION SUMMARY: 2001 FREELANDER ENGINES

1.8i

1,796cc in-line four-cylinder (80mm bore x 89.3mm stroke) K-series petrol with alloy block and head, mounted transversely
Two belt-driven overhead camshafts, four valves per cylinder, 10.5:1 compression ratio
Multi-point sequential fuel injection system
Electronic management by MEMS 3.0 ECU
Maximum power: 115bhp at 5,500rpm
Maximum torque: 118lb ft at 2,750rpm

These later versions of the 1.8-litre K-series petrol engine had been modified for the 2001 model-year to meet the new and tighter EU3 emissions regulations. The modifications brought slightly lower outputs at the same crankshaft speeds as the earlier engines. These engines were manufactured for Land Rover by Powertrain Limited.

Td4

1,951cc four-cylinder (84mm bore x 88mm stroke) with iron block and alloy head, mounted transversely
Two chain-driven overhead camshafts, four valves per cylinder
Common-rail high-pressure fuel system with direct injection
Turbocharged and intercooled
Electronic management by Bosch DDE 4.0 system
Maximum power: 112bhp at 4,000rpm
Maximum torque: 192lb ft at 1,750rpm

Designed by BMW and manufactured at Steyr in Austria, the Td4 is a version of the company's M47 engine which was announced at the Geneva Motor Show in March 1997.

Although the cylinder blocks are made of cast iron, the design saves weight by incorporating hollow stiffening beams into the casting. The Bosch engine management system is a fully electronic (drive-by-wire) type, and controls fuelling, turbocharger boost and Exhaust Gas Recirculation (EGR).

V6

2,497cc six-cylinder in 90° V formation (80mm bore x 82.8mm stroke) with alloy block and head, mounted transversely
Four belt-driven overhead camshafts, four valves per cylinder, 10.5:1 compression ratio
Multipoint sequential fuel injection system
Electronic management by Siemens 2000 ECU
Maximum power: 175bhp at 6,250rpm
Maximum torque: 177lb ft at 4,000rpm

Like the four-cylinder K-series, the KV6 engine was a Rover design which was manufactured for Land Rover by Powertrain Limited. A Siemens management system controls fuelling, idle speed, ignition, the Variable Induction System, the main radiator fans and the fuel pump.

Fuel would be delivered to the combustion chambers by the very latest in electronically controlled, high-pressure, common-rail injection technology which further improved fuel efficiency. In addition, the plan was to improve high-speed performance by using four valves per cylinder like the latest high-performance petrol engines, rather than the traditional two valves per cylinder. Four-cylinder engines would thus become what marketing departments love to call '16-valve' types, but the BMW diesels would have an important and unique characteristic. Instead of all four valves being directly above the cylinder, there would be just three – two exhaust valves and one inlet, the latter with a helical high-swirl port. The second inlet valve would be at the side of the combustion chamber. The results were vastly improved intake swirl characteristics and more efficient combustion.

Two basic engines were under development: one a V8 design and the other an in-line type which could be produced with either four or six cylinders. The new six-cylinder was quickly snapped up by the Land Rover team working on the next new Range Rover, and appeared in that vehicle during 2002. The four-cylinder, with its planned capacity of around 2.0 litres, was an obvious choice for the Freelander. It was also chosen by the team then working on the next new Rover saloon, and became the power unit for diesel versions of that car which was announced in 1998.

The four-cylinder turbocharged diesel was known to BMW as the M47 engine and was announced in March 1997 at the Geneva Show as the power unit of the brand-new E46 series 320d models. It featured chain-driven twin overhead camshafts in place of the belt-driven camshafts of earlier BMW diesels, an alloy cylinder head and iron block, and had a swept volume of 1,951cc. Both turbocharged and intercooled, it offered instantaneous cold-starting except in temperatures below freezing – an advance over the Freelander's Rover-built L-series diesel which always needed a few seconds while its glow-plugs warmed the combustion chambers. Most exciting, though, was its advanced Variable Nozzle Turbine (VNT) technology.

VNT altered the pitch of the turbocharger's vanes to maximise the effect of the exhaust gases at lower engine speeds. At low speeds when there was little gas flow, the vanes were turned fully into the exhaust stream. At high speeds, when more gas was passing across the turbines, the vanes were turned less. The result was a nearly constant turbocharger effect, without the usual flat off-boost response. The pitch of the vanes was controlled by the Bosch DDE 4.0 electronic engine management system, which also controlled fuelling and the Exhaust Gas Recirculation (EGR) system.

However, the Freelander version of the engine had a number of fundamental differences from the BMW unit as first seen in that company's 320d saloons. For a start, it was installed transversely, while the BMW saloons had the engine mounted north-south. It also had a structural cast alloy sump which incorporated the lower torque reaction arm of the transverse installation.

In addition, the Land Rover version of the engine had a different state of tune, delivering 110bhp at 4,000rpm and 192lb ft at 1,750rpm. The BMW 320d, by contrast, had 136bhp at 4,000rpm and 206lb ft at 2,000rpm – but these peak figures do not tell the whole story, as the Land Rover version of the engine had been tuned to deliver a different spread of torque as well. One interesting characteristic of the Td4 engine was that it proved slow to warm up in the Freelander, and was therefore accompanied by a Webasto fuel-burning heater which speeded cabin warm-up by heating the coolant water independently of the engine.

While the M47 engine – which Land Rover would market as the Td4 – would make the diesel Freelander perform better, it was also important to push the envelope of Freelander performance to a greater extent by introducing a high-performance petrol engine. Rover Cars were continuing to develop the 1.8-litre K-series, but there was little doubt that serious performance enthusiasts would only be attracted to the Freelander if it had a big-capacity engine on offer.

The KV6 petrol engine

This requirement had been envisaged right from the start of serious work on the CB40 project, and so the vehicle's engine bay had been designed to accommodate a larger engine – which explains why the four-cylinders tend to look somewhat lost in all that space under the bonnet! There was an obvious candidate here, too. Rover Cars had been developing a V6 derivative of the K-series engine, expanding that family upwards from its largest 1.8-litre size as far as 2.5 litres and perhaps beyond. Like the four-cylinder 1.8-litre K-series and the four-cylinder 2.0-litre L-series diesel, the KV6 was designed for transverse installation, so its use brought no need for fundamental changes to the rest of the Freelander's driveline.

In the late 1980s and early 1990s, V6 engines had gained in popularity for the 2-litre to 3-litre class, as

The V6 petrol engine filled the Freelander's engine bay much more successfully than the 1.8-litre K-series had done.

This is what the V6 engine looked like out of the vehicle. As with all Freelander engines, it was mounted transversely.

Mud-spattered after a spot of gentle off-road driving, this is the 1.8-litre petrol engine in a 2001 model-year Freelander. It was essentially the same as the earlier 1.8-litre type, but modified to meet new emissions regulations and reduce servicing requirements.

they offered compact dimensions which enabled a large-capacity engine to be accommodated in an engine bay where a smaller-capacity four-cylinder engine was a snug fit. Rover's initial aim in developing their V6 – known, not surprisingly, as the KV6 – was to replace the Honda V6 in their 800-series cars, but of course they anticipated that the engine would have further uses elsewhere. They introduced it in Rover 825 models in 1996, and later used it in other saloons, with both the original 2.5-litre and the later 2.0-litre swept volumes.

Therefore, when development work on the V6-engined Freelander began in 1996, the basic engine installation was straightforward. Tests showed up engine cooling problems, however, and the only way around this was to improve airflow by redesigning the front end of the vehicle. In addition, V6-equipped

Although the V6 model's extended nose was hard to spot, the ribbed air intake panel was instantly recognisable. Note also the clear indicator lenses on this three-door Softback.

Freelanders behaved differently in frontal impact tests from the existing four-cylinder models. The front end structure had to be re-engineered to cope, and the V6 models ended up with a different bumper and front apron assembly from the four-cylinder types.

In developing the V6 Freelander, though, there was to be one more fly in the ointment. Once the plan to develop a high-performance variant with the KV6 engine became more widely known within the company, it appears that Land Rover North America started to take an interest. As explained in Chapter Two, the Americans had declined to take the original Freelander, arguing that it would not appeal to their customers. However, a 177bhp 2.5-litre model was quite a different matter: they decided that they would be able to market one of those, and the sooner the better.

The result was that the North American requirement had to be grafted on to the KV6 Freelander development programme – and because of the late start, North America did not get its Freelander until two years after the V6 models went on sale in other markets. Some sources insist that the front end of the Freelander had to be redesigned not only to improve cooling for the V6 engine but also to meet tough American crash regulations – but it has so far proved impossible to get a straight answer out of Land Rover on that issue.

Although the architecture of the KV6 forbade the through-bolt construction of the in-line K-series four-cylinders, the engine did borrow their use of a stiffening ladder-frame around the crankshaft bearings, and shared their ultra-compact bore spacing.

Despite the use of twin overhead camshafts for each cylinder bank to operate four valves per cylinder, width was minimised by driving each exhaust camshaft from the rear of the corresponding inlet camshaft, so allowing smaller drivewheels and a shorter toothed belt. Meanwhile, an electronically controlled Variable Induction System (VIS), using separate plenum chambers and throttles for each bank of cylinders, allowed both strong mid-range full-load torque characteristics, and improved part-load fuel economy.

The KV6 has always had a distributorless ignition system, with an individual coil for each cylinder. Freelander versions of the engine, developed to meet the EU3 emissions regulations, use a Siemens 2000 ECU and have specially shaped downpipes to give a characteristic exhaust note. Each downpipe also incorporates a starter catalyst to minimise emissions during warm-up.

New transmissions

Just as BMW engine technology was state-of-the-art in the mid-1990s, so BMW transmission design led the rest of the motor industry. Most notable, perhaps, was its Steptronic gearshift system, introduced in 1996. This was available with the five-speed ZF automatic gearboxes in BMW saloons, and combined the convenience of automatic transmission with the precise and individual control of a manual gearbox. It was, in effect, the best of both worlds.

Steptronic provided fully automatic gearchanging in a conventional P-R-N-D gate, but alongside that (to its

Left top: New badging distinguished one model from another, although the 1.8-litre petrol models still had no identification on the tail door. This is the 'Td4' badge . . .

Left bottom: . . . and this is the 'V6' badge. There were also trim-level identification badges on the front wings . . .

Below: . . . as seen here.

right in both LHD and RHD models) was a second operating gate. This was marked with a plus sign above it and a minus sign below. Moving the lever forwards to the plus position against light spring pressure shifted up a gear, and moving the lever backwards to the minus position gave a downchange.

There were built-in safeguards, of course. The system ignored commands to shift down a gear if the road speed was too high, and it automatically changed up a gear just before the governed maximum engine speed if the driver failed to do so. In addition, on BMWs Steptronic automatically shifted down to fourth or to third gear if the driver checked the car's speed with the brakes, so that instant acceleration was always available from a touch on the accelerator pedal.

The Land Rover engineers decided that they wanted a Steptronic control system for automatic versions of the revised Freelanders. However, they decided against using the ZF automatic gearboxes that BMW favoured, plumping instead for the Japanese-made JATCO five-speed automatics as used in some Rover cars. The Freelander system included a 'Sport' programme which was selected automatically in Steptronic mode and allowed higher revs for better acceleration and earlier downchanges for faster response. It also incorporated sophisticated adaptive programming, which recognised situations such as towing, downhill overrun, steep mountain roads and high altitudes, and selected the optimum shift strategies for each.

The automatic-with-Steptronic transmission was made standard for V6-engined Freelanders, with no alternative. It was made optional with the new Td4 diesel engine, which came as standard with a five-speed manual gearbox made by Getrag in Germany – another company with which BMW enjoyed a close relationship. However, there would be no automatic option for the entry-level four-cylinder petrol Freelanders.

The 2001 models

These, then, were the major changes which were announced for the 2001-model Freelanders that went on sale in September 2000. The two new engines were accompanied by a revised version of the 1.8-litre K-series four-cylinder petrol unit, giving a choice of three different powerplants. Three-door Softback and Hardback bodies, plus the five-door Station Wagon, made up the other major choices for Freelander buyers – but the 2001 models also incorporated a large number of other important changes.

When the Steptronic automatic transmission was fitted, this was the gearshift which greeted the driver. Selector positions are marked on the driver's side, and this is a RHD vehicle.

That revised K-series engine brought no real surprises. Now known as the '1.8i' type to distinguish it from the earlier 1.8-litre (although Land Rover were never very consistent about this nomenclature), it had been re-tuned to meet the latest EU3 emissions regulations. A 'starter catalyst' built into the exhaust manifold down-pipe minimised emissions during warm-up, but overall there was a slight loss of power and torque as compared with the earlier engine.

The 1.8i had a new and more powerful engine ECU called MEMS 3, which allowed full sequential injection. It also boasted a direct, distributorless, ignition with two twin-output, plug-top coils. A new camshaft sensor provided the precise positional information required for the new injection and ignition systems, while new automatic tensioners for the cam belt and the alternator-and-air conditioner pump belt gave quieter running. They also extended the cam belt service life from 60,000 to 90,000 miles.

Like the Td4 and V6 power units, the 1.8i had a new 'torque axis' mounting system. This used two hydraulically damped engine mounts – 'Hydramounts' – to carry the engine mass. These were positioned on the

COLOURS AND TRIMS

2001 model-year (September 2000 to August 2001)

A range of 14 paint finishes was offered for the 2001 model-year. New colours Monte Carlo Blue and Oslo Blue replaced Cobar Blue and Oxford Blue, while Bonatti Grey was an additional option. There were again two solid and three metallic colours, while the remaining nine were micatallics.

As before, certain interior trim combinations were 'recommended' (i.e. standard) although the alternative interior colour was always available to special order. Three-door models still had a choice of Teal or Smokestone upholstery in Jungle fabric, while five-doors came with a choice of Smokestone or Dark Smokestone Tapestry fabrics. Leather upholstery on three-doors combined panels of Teal and Smokestone colours, while on five-doors it combined Light and Dark Smokestone.

The combinations were as follows:

Alveston Red (micatallic)	Smokestone (all models)
Appalachian Green (micatallic)	Smokestone (3-dr) or Dark Smokestone (5-dr)
Blenheim Silver (metallic)	Smokestone (3-dr) or Dark Smokestone (5-dr)
Bonatti Grey (metallic)	Smokestone (all models)
Chawton White (solid)	Teal (3-dr) or Dark Smokestone (5-dr)
Epsom Green (micatallic)	Smokestone (all models)
Icelandic Blue (micatallic)	Teal (3-dr) or Smokestone (5-dr)
Java Black (micatallic)	Teal (3-dr) or Dark Smokestone (5-dr)
Kent Green (micatallic)	Smokestone (3-dr) or Dark Smokestone (5-dr)
Kinversand (micatallic)	Smokestone (3-dr) or Dark Smokestone (5-dr)
Monte Carlo Blue (micatallic)	Smokestone (all models)
Oslo Blue (micatallic)	Smokestone (all models)
Rutland Red (solid)	Smokestone (all models)
White Gold (metallic)	Smokestone (all models)

torque axis, which is the axis around which the engine would naturally tend to rotate if unrestrained. At the top and bottom, each engine was restrained by torque reaction rods. This configuration gave an excellent combination of power unit 'ride' control and isolation of noise, vibration and harshness problems.

However, it would be easy on a superficial look to dismiss the 2001 model-year enhancements as purely related to the drivetrain. In fact, they went far deeper: Land Rover boasted that the new or modified

VIN CODES FOR FREELANDERS (2001 MODEL-YEAR)

The VIN codes used in this period consisted of 17 characters, made up of an 11-character prefix code and a six-digit serial number.

Example: SALLNAAA71A-123456.

This breaks down as follows:

SAL	Manufacturer code (Rover Group)	
LN	Freelander	
A	Standard trim	
	B =	Commercial trim
A	Three-door body (Hardback or Softback)	
	B =	Five-door body (Station Wagon)
A	1.8-litre K-series petrol engine (HOU spec)	
	C =	1.8-litre K-series petrol engine (LOU spec)
	D =	1.8-litre K-series petrol engine (LOL spec)
	E =	2.0-litre Td4 diesel engine
	F =	1.8-litre K-series petrol engine (HOL spec)
	G =	2.5-litre V6 petrol engine (for unleaded fuel)
	H =	2.5-litre V6 petrol engine (for leaded fuel)
	J =	2.5-litre V6 petrol engine (for ethanol fuel)
1	RHD with 5-speed Steptronic automatic gearbox	
	2 =	LHD with 5-speed Steptronic automatic gearbox
	7 =	RHD with 5-speed manual gearbox
	8 =	LHD with 5-speed manual gearbox
1	Model-year 2001	
A	Assembled at Solihull	
123456	Serial number	

component count ranged from 40 per cent on the 1.8i models to some 70 per cent on a top-specification V6 or Td4.

New colours aside – and there were three for 2001, as the sidebar shows – the 2001 models could be distinguished by their clear front direction indicators, integrating with the headlamps to make the vehicle look wider. The Td4 and 1.8-litre petrol models had a revised front bumper design with an enlarged lower air intake, while the V6 versions had a 65mm longer front bumper assembly, incorporating airflow management ducting for the uprated cooling system. The body-colour section of the front apron also incorporated a distinctive castellated profile.

The original (and rather confusing) designations of entry-level i or di, mid-range Xi or Xdi, and top-level XEi or XEdi were abandoned. In their place came entry-level S, mid-range GS and top-model ES types – a

The Freelander V6 Sport limited edition featured the 2001 model-year twin auxiliary lamp pods. Just visible here is the 'Sport' identifying badge below the side repeater indicator on the front wing.

three-tier range once again, but this time using the designations already familiar from the Land Rover Discovery range. All models were in fact better equipped than earlier types, the ES trim level introducing a new level of luxury to the Freelander range, with such things as heated seats, power-fold door mirrors, a six-disc CD autochanger as standard, and twin illuminated vanity mirrors. The 2001 Freelanders wore identifying badges, too: the Td4 and V6 models carried those letters on the tail door, and there were S, GS or ES letters for the front wings. However, these letters could be deleted at the customer's request.

As for wheels – a vital element in model differentiation by the start of the 21st century – the entry-level models still had 15-inch styled steel types with 195 tyres. The GS models came with 16-inch Adventure six-spoke alloys and 195 tyres, while Td4 and 1.8 ES types had 16-inch Freedom five-spoke alloys on 215 tyres. Only the V6 ES came with 16-inch Triple Sport alloys that had three split spokes and ran on 215 tyres – but options and accessories meant that these elements were not an infallible guide for small boys and keen fathers to distinguish one Freelander from another.

All wheels had extra clearance to accommodate the larger, 277mm, brake discs which replaced the earlier 262mm size on the 2001 models. These discs were now ventilated as well, and were matched by wider rear drums and an improved parking brake actuation. The four-channel ABS system became standard on all

variants, and was of a new type made by Teves. It was smoother and quieter than the earlier Bosch type, and in addition to ETC and HDC it incorporated Electronic Brakeforce Distribution (EBD). Suspension revisions included larger-diameter struts, plus revised damping, geometry and bushing, while the power-assisted steering had new valving and a higher operating pressure for improved response.

Inside the vehicle, larger airbags were fitted in preparation for the North American launch of Freelander (European regulations allow a smaller-capacity bag than the one demanded in North America). All models had a new and more powerful heating-and-ventilating system, and there was a new and improved air-conditioning system as well, which was standard on GS and ES models.

Cabin enhancements for all models included a new high centre console with a stowage box, improved ash trays and the auxiliary power socket which was formerly an option. Station Wagons gained electric rear windows as standard, a 'one-shot-down' driver's window, an upgraded six-speaker radio-cassette system and extra soundproofing. A new immobilisation system added extra protection against theft while digital multiplex electronics allowed faster communication between the various ECUs positioned around the vehicle.

WORLD RALLY SUPPORT VEHICLES

Six Freelander V6 models were specially prepared as recce vehicles for the Ford World Rally Car team's entry in the Safari Rally, held in Kenya during July 2001.

The vehicles were used in the reconnaissance period before the rally when the drivers and co-drivers drove over the rally stages to produce and check pace notes. Each vehicle covered a distance of approximately 4,000km at high speeds in only three days.

The Freelanders were prepared by M-Sport, who built that year's Ford Focus World Rally Cars for Ford Racing. Their bodyshells were seam-welded and strengthened in key areas, and a custom-built M-Sport roll cage was integrated into the main stress points. Additional strengthening went into the 'chassis', and strut braces were fitted front and rear.

Externally, the World Rally Freelanders featured a safari-specification brush bar with mounts for additional spotlights. The brush bar also supported a full-length, rally-specification aluminium sump guard. Kevlar sill protectors and a rear differential guard were also added.

To combat the extreme underbonnet temperatures in Africa, a bonnet vent and additional transmission oil coolers were fitted. A new air-box was designed, and an external snorkel fitted for deep wading. All windows were covered with a reflective film to help the air conditioning system to maintain a comfortable temperature inside the vehicles, and a high-capacity windscreen washer bottle was fitted.

The wheels were custom-made by OZ Racing and ran on Pirelli tyres. Each vehicle carried two spare wheels stowed inside. The suspension was made fully adjustable, with strengthened links, cross-members and arms, while engine and gearbox mounts were also toughened up.

A large 120-litre bag-tank with a carbon cover was fitted inside each vehicle to improve the range, and two dry cell batteries were fitted to achieve a more even weight distribution. The interior featured two Sparco carbon Kevlar seats with six-point harnesses, as used in the rally cars. The dashboard had an additional anti-glare coating and there was navigation equipment and even a fridge to keep drinking water cold.

The World Rally Freelanders were not part of a development programme specific to Freelander, but there can be little doubt that the lessons learned from their use in this testing environment were fed back into the design teams for possible future use.

Five vehicles were fitted with 2004-model front and rear details and repainted for the 2004 Freelander press launch (see page 6). The sixth car, unrebuilt, was used as a safety car in the 2003 British Rally Championship.

V6 Freelanders were used as recce vehicles by the Ford Focus World Rally Team in 2001.

Chapter **Six**

2002 and beyond

Moving up-market

Once Land Rover had decided to take the Freelander into the North American market, the vehicle had to be developed to meet the expectations and needs of that region's customers. The introduction of the 2.5-litre V6 petrol engine on 2001 models was just the first step; after that, additional equipment and a more luxurious specification had to be developed to go along with Land Rover's 'premium product' image in North America.

The success of those V6 models confirmed there were plenty of customers outside North America who were prepared to pay a little more for a top-of-the-range Freelander. So the obvious next step was to load these top models with more equipment, which could also be fitted to the smaller-engined types in countries where demand existed.

It made sense, then, to develop the specification enhancements for North America in tandem with those for the rest of the world, and both requirements were wrapped up in the 2002 model-year Freelander programme. However, not all the refinements developed for the 2002 NAS (North American Specification) Freelanders were made available on 2002 models for other countries; some were held over until the 2003 model-year. For this reason, the NAS Freelanders are dealt with separately, in Chapter Seven.

The 2002 models

Pre-launch publicity activities for the NAS Freelanders allowed customers in that market to see some of the 2002 model-year changes well before they were announced for other markets. However, the official launch of the 2002-model Freelanders was at the Frankfurt International Motor Show in Germany, which opened on 11 September 2001. Their new features included exterior styling changes, revisions to the interior trim and improvements in equipment levels.

The most obvious change for the 2002 Freelanders was that all the exterior grey plastic mouldings had been changed to black. This meant new bumpers, wheelarches, sill finishers, tail door cladding and fuel

DID YOU KNOW?

Only in Scotland – the Braemar

Land Rover dealers in Scotland were able to offer a special-edition Freelander which was not available anywhere else in the third quarter of 2001. The Freelander Braemar was announced at the Scottish Motor Show on 9 November 2001, and was based on either the 1.8S Hardback (£16,995) or the 1.8GS Station Wagon (£19,495).

The Braemar was a special edition sold through Scottish dealers in late 2001 as a 2002 model.

All vehicles had Blenheim Silver paint, privacy glass, side rubbing strips, front and rear lamp guards, and 17-inch Triple Sport alloy wheels. There were 30 of the three-door models, all fitted with roof rails, split rear seats, front and rear mud flaps, a wheel nut kit and a single-CD player. The 40 Station Wagons had a CD autochanger.

There were also Braemar editions of the Defender, Discovery and Range Rover.

The key visual change for the 2002 model-year was the use of black body protection mouldings in place of the earlier grey.

The black theme was continued inside, where the fascia and centre console were also given new black mouldings – although the basic shape of the dash remained unchanged.

filler cap – and, of course, the hardback on three-door models which had one. The rear direction indicator lenses also changed from amber to a smoke-effect finish.

New colours were Vienna Green (replacing Kent Green) and Zambezi Silver (replacing Blenheim Silver), and there was a new range of alloy wheels. The 16-inch

WHEEL OPTIONS, 2002

For the 2002 model-year, no fewer than nine different wheel options were available for Freelander models.

15-inch	Styled steel (five-spoke)
	Adventure alloy (six-spoke)
16-inch	Freedom alloy (five-spoke)
	Active alloy (five-spoke)
	Triple Sport alloy (three paired spokes)
17-inch	Freedom alloy (six-spoke; accessory fit only)
	TRek alloy (six-spoke)
	Evolution alloy (three paired spokes)
	Triple Sport alloy (three paired spokes; accessory fit only)

DID YOU KNOW?

The three-millionth Land Rover

A North American specification Freelander was chosen to become the 3,000,000th Land Rover at a short ceremony held in the Solihull factory on Monday, 1 October 2001.

It was driven off the assembly line in the early afternoon by singing star Ronan Keating, a confirmed Land Rover enthusiast. Keating added his congratulations to a speech by manufacturing director Marin Burela. 'This is a great day for Land Rover,' said Burela. 'It is also a tribute to all the people who have worked at Land Rover over the years, and to the current workforce.'

The Monte Carlo Blue vehicle carried US-style VIN SALNY2222A-357498, and its European-style VIN (found only on in-house paperwork) was SALLNABG22A-357498. It was not retained at the factory but was shipped to the USA for sale in the normal way.

The three-millionth Land Rover was a 2002 model-year North American Specification (NAS) Freelander, and was driven off the line by singing star Ronan Keating.

The figure of 3,000,000 Land Rovers was calculated by adding together production totals for Land Rover utilities (since 1948), Range Rovers (since 1970), Discoverys (since 1989) and Freelanders (since 1997). By the time this vehicle was built, Freelander production stood at over 250,000 examples.

These dash-mounted cupholders were new for 2002, but were optional outside North America. This all-black dash is on a 2003 model.

The raised centre console cubby introduced on 2001 models is seen here on a 2002-model North American Freelander, with leather upholstery.

Active style was for 1.8-litre models, while the 17-inch TRek style became optional for both 1.8i and Td4 models. The 17-inch Evolution wheel was an option for V6 models only.

Inside, the existing Smokestone trim colour was supplemented by Black, which was available for the seats in cloth, leather, or Alcantara-and-leather. Black could be combined with pale beige Alpaca on top-of-the-range models only to give a high-contrast style with what Land Rover described as a contemporary feel. The Black-and-Alpaca seats had a special new sports

KIT-BUILT FREELANDERS

The process of shipping vehicles in kit form to be assembled overseas is one which motor manufacturers have used for many years. It was originally introduced as a means of selling a product in an overseas territory where trade or tax barriers would have made its price prohibitive in fully-built form. Typically, a country keen to protect its domestic economy might impose high taxation on imported cars while attempting to kick-start its own motor manufacturing industry. However, the chance of training local labour in car manufacture by assembling the products of an overseas manufacturer is an arrangement which suits all parties. Often, the deal involves a staged increase in the quantity of locally sourced parts, leading eventually to full local manufacture under licence from the original manufacturer.

The first Land Rovers to be assembled in this way left Solihull in what is called CKD (completely knocked-down) from as early as August 1949, and the company has continued to use both this method and SKD (semi-knocked-down – where the vehicle is shipped in larger sub-assemblies), ever since.

The first CKD operation for Freelanders was opened in Thailand, where this picture was taken. A similar operation in South Africa followed.

The first country to build Freelanders from KD kits was Thailand, where assembly operations began in November 2001. The vehicles were built on dedicated body framing and final lines at the assembly plant of Land Rover's Premier Automotive Group partner Volvo, near Bangkok. Other manufacturing resources and facilities, including the paint shop, were shared with Volvo products.

A second Freelander KD operation was established in South Africa, at the existing Land Rover KD plant in Silverton, owned by Ford, over the summer of 2002. A proportion of the vehicles built there were shipped to Australia (where the Freelander was not selling very strongly), but a number of early examples were reported to have faulty paintwork.

THE DUTCH FREELANDER COMMERCIAL

Road tax regulations in the Netherlands demand that vehicles registered as 'commercial' types should have certain minimum dimensions in the load-carrying area behind the seats. Further regulations cover such things as windows in the load area and the type of bulkhead fitted between this and the driving compartment.

The Dutch Freelander Commercial.

There are substantial benefits to meeting the requirements of the tax definition of a 'commercial' in Holland. Vehicles which do so are taxed at a very much lower rate than others, with the effect that vans and other commercial types which do not meet the regulations are virtually unsaleable in that country.

As few manufacturers outside the Netherlands produce vehicles with the right specification, there is scope for domestic coachbuilders to modify imported vehicles to meet the regulations. Typically, these modifications will involve raising the roof and fitting or altering the bulkhead between load area and driving compartment. 'Commercial' versions of the Land Rover Discovery were built by Ter Berg bv with a distinctive raised roof and other modifications, and with the full approval of Land Rover's importers.

The Freelander Commercial as built by Land Rover Special Vehicles and introduced in 1999 (see Chapter Four) did not meet the Dutch criteria for a tax-reduced 'commercial' and was therefore not sold in that country. However, in 2002 at the RAI Show in Amsterdam, Land Rover displayed a Dutch-market Freelander Commercial with a specially raised rear roof section which enabled it to meet local regulations for 'commercials'. These vehicles are converted in the Netherlands and have only ever been available in that country.

design, with new foams, revised headrests, longer side bolsters and an extra 15mm of cushion length to improve support and comfort. They were matched by Alpaca door casings and door pulls, a black leather-trimmed steering wheel and a new beige carpet.

The centre console and instrument binnacle meanwhile became black with all colours. The old Teal Blue used for air vents, heater surrounds and speaker surrounds gave way to Gunmetal on three-door models and Black on five-doors. All Freelanders also had a new and supposedly more sporty-looking instrument pack with new graphics – which, it later turned out, shared their style with the one used on the third-generation Range Rover, which would be introduced at the turn of the year. The new instrument pack also incorporated a microprocessor that enabled the driver to monitor vehicle functions and acted as a 'gateway' for information flowing between vehicle systems.

Optional were new front and rear cupholders, designed primarily to suit the large-capacity paper or plastic cups typically supplied by fast-food outlets in North America. The front one folded away into the centre of the dash top, and the rear one retracted into the centre armrest.

The base in-car entertainment package was now a CD-compatible head unit with six speakers, while a new premium head unit with single-CD capability was added to the range. At the top of the range, a Harman Kardon-branded system featured the premium head unit, an additional power amplifier, remote controls on the steering wheel, and a nine-speaker sound system including a sub-woofer. A Becker satellite navigation system was also on offer, packaged in a DIN-sized head unit that offered premium sound quality plus a dual-mode CD player that could interpret both navigation and audio CDs.

There was also one cost-saving deletion. Td4-engined Freelanders for 2002 lost the Webasto fuel-burning heater which had been fitted as standard to 2001 models to speed warming of the passenger compartment. This was replaced by an electric coil-type heater.

Meanwhile, the Steptronic automatic transmission was rebranded as CommandShift with effect from October 2001 – although it took some time for the new name to make its mark. Exactly why this was done is not clear, but the most likely reason is that the Steptronic name was associated with BMW and that Ford (who now owned Land Rover) wanted to impose their own identity on it.

A TUNED Td4 FOR GERMAN CUSTOMERS

Another example of a special-edition Freelander unique to an overseas market was provided by the Freelander Black Spirit sold through selected German Land Rover dealers in late 2002.

The key feature of this special edition was that its Td4 engine had been rechipped by well-known German tuning specialist AC Schnitzer to deliver 129PS (instead of the standard 112PS) and 320Nm of torque (as against the standard 260Nm). The German monthly *Alles Allrad* reported that 0–62mph in the Black Spirit with CommandShift automatic gearbox took 13.8 seconds (standard 15.7sec) while maximum speed was 174km/h (108mph) (standard 166km/h – 103mph). The bad news was that fuel consumption increased, from the standard 9.0 litres to 9.3 litres per 100km.

It looked standard, but this German special-edition Freelander, Black Spirit, had a rechipped Td4 diesel engine. Badging was very discreet, as usual – look under the side repeaters if you can't see it!

All 400 vehicles were Station Wagons, finished in Java Black and fitted with air conditioning and a radio with CD player. The wheels were 17-inch TRek alloys fitted with 225/55R17 tyres, but there were two levels of equipment. There were 320 vehicles with five-speed manual gearboxes and black cloth upholstery, with a further 80 with CommandShift automatic transmissions and leather-and-Alcantara upholstery.

MORE GERMAN SPECIAL EDITIONS

The early months of 2003 saw two more special-edition Freelanders for the German market. Known as the Freelander Style and the Freelander Rock, both of them featured body-coloured bumpers, aprons and wheelarch protection mouldings.

Also standard were air conditioning, six-spoke alloy wheels and a CD player. The Style, which came as a Hardback three-door or a Station Wagon, also had leather upholstery. The Rock was promoted as a more sporty edition.

Prices started at 23,900 Euros for the Rock and 25,600 Euros for the Style.

The 2003 models

The Freelander entered the 2003 model-year with a further set of revisions, some of them based on changes already previewed on the North American models during 2002. The 2003 European models were first displayed at the Paris Motor Show which opened on 26 September 2002, but the UK-specification variants – which had minor differences and included some special editions – were not announced until the British International Motor Show at Birmingham's National Exhibition Centre in October.

The only external identifier on the 2003 models was what Land Rover described as '3D' badging. The basic range of S, GS and ES models was supplemented by a new top-of-the-range model. In the UK, this was badged as an ES Premium, while for Continental Europe and other markets it carried the HSE badging used on top-model Freelanders for North America. Its introduction reflected growing demand for better-specified Freelanders, and of course allowed Land Rover to close the gap between the most expensive Freelanders and the entry-level Discoverys.

Models with 15-inch wheels had a new All-season tyre to improve on-road ride, handling and refinement, while other wheel sizes retained their All-terrain tyres. All V6-engined models took on a larger petrol tank with revised fuel pick-up point, which was claimed to extend their range between fill-ups by 10 per cent.

What Land Rover described as '3D' badging was new for all the 2003 models, and the rebranding of Steptronic as CommandShift was made universal.

Like the 2003 Discoverys, the 2003 Freelanders were given a new all-black fascia, thus completing the gradual change from grey and blue which had begun on the 2002 models. The Black and Smokestone alternative colourways for the interior trim remained unchanged, but a new fan and ducting in the heating and ventilating system improved airflow and reduced fan noise.

The new ES Premium (or HSE) model was available only as a five-door Station Wagon, and came as standard with the premium sports seats in black and pale beige Alpaca, the matching two-tone steering wheel, and carpets, door casings and door pulls in Alpaca Beige. Meanwhile, the Harman Kardon ICE was a standard fit, and the HSE also came with the front and rear cupholders as standard. Both ES and ES Premium models could be ordered with the option of a black side rubbing strip to protect the vehicle from car park knocks.

There were changes in the options availability for 2003 as well. For the Td4 models, the fuel-burning heater which had been fitted as standard on 2001 models but deleted for 2002 was reintroduced as an extra-cost option. It was offered as part of an option pack with the heated windscreen (previously available only on V6 models), and for Td4 GS models it was possible to buy an option pack which combined the

THE FREELANDER ESX

The Freelander ESX was introduced to the UK market in September 2001 to give a boost to sales of the then-new 2002 models. It was a five-door Station Wagon which was available in any one of five colours: Biarritz Blue (unique to the model), Alveston Red, Java Black, Monte Carlo Blue or Zambezi Silver. There were 500 examples in all, of which 100 had the 1.8-litre petrol engine, 150 came with the V6, and the lion's share of 250 examples had the Td4 diesel engine.

Special editions helped to keep Freelander sales up, although the vehicle had by this stage lost its place as the best-selling 4x4 in Europe. This limited-edition Station Wagon was called the ESX, and was announced at the start of the 2002 model-year. Note the badging below the side repeater lamp.

According to Freelander marketing manager, Naveen Dayal, 'The newest Land Rover is ideal for young business executives who want to be noticed on a crowded street. It is a vehicle that offers no compromise or restriction for the driver who wants to go anywhere.'

The ESX came with an accessories pack which included an electric sunroof, power-fold body-colour door mirrors, 17-inch Freedom alloy wheels, metallic paint, air conditioning, roof rails, mud flaps, a passenger airbag, black side runners, front and rear lamp guards and a soft-feel black nudge bar. Td4 models had single auxiliary lamp pods while V6 versions were distinguished by double lamp pods.

French special editions for 2002 included the Freelander 360°, in both three-door and Station Wagon forms . . .

FRENCH SPECIAL EDITIONS, 2002–2003

Land Rover's National Sales Companies in different countries around the world do not always sell vehicles with the same specification as the mainstream home-market models. Although it is not possible to list every single variant worldwide here, it is interesting to see what Land Rover France came up with in the way of special editions during 2002 and 2003.

The company brought two special-edition Freelanders to market during the 2002 season. First was the Freelander Tecnica, a 250-strong limited edition launched at the beginning of 2002 in collaboration with Tecnica, the Italian sports equipment manufacturer. This was available only with the 1.8-litre engine, but as either a three-door or a five-door model. The Freelander Tecnica came with 15-inch Advantage alloy wheels, a Smokestone leather interior and (for just 0.15 Euros extra) a pair of Tecnica Rival X7 Ultrafit ski boots.

For Summer 2002, the limited edition was called the Freelander 360°. Based on the latest Freelander SX model with either Td4 or V6 engine, this could be had with either manual (Td4 only) or automatic (both) transmission, and with either three-door or five-door body.

There were 500 of these models, all with leather seats (in black or beige), a VDO Dayton MS 4200 satnav system combined with the ICE, and certain other items of special equipment. Each vehicle carried a green and chrome 'Freelander 360°' badge below the rear number plate. Buying the limited edition models saved 2,340 Euros over buying a standard model and equipping it to the same level.

From September 2002, French Land Rover buyers were offered the special-edition Freelander Arusha. This was a 1,500-strong edition of three-door and five-door models with a choice of either the Td4 or 1.8i engine. Td4s could be had with manual or CommandShift gearboxes. There were wood or aluminium-finish dashboard highlights, an Arusha logo on the dash and an RDS radio with CD player and steering wheel controls. The silver bodywork was complemented by a hard wheel cover in black and chrome, plus grilles over the front light units.

. . . and the Freelander Arusha, which was much more distinctive as long as it was wearing its special spare wheel cover.

heated windscreen with the heated front seats already standard on ES and ES Premium derivatives.

Mid-year revisions

During 2002, the popularity of Td4-powered Freelanders increased at the expense of the 1.8-litre petrol models. So, in January 2003, Land Rover UK introduced a revised and stronger Td4 range to maintain the Freelander's sales edge over new diesel competitors.

The top and bottom models of the old Td4 range continued, with the S models offering an entry-level

2003 UK LIMITED EDITIONS – SERENGETI AND KALAHARI

Land Rover introduced two new limited-edition derivatives of the 1.8-litre Freelander for the UK market in September 2002, a few weeks in advance of their appearance at the British International Motor Show in October. These were known as the Serengeti and the Kalahari.

The Serengeti was based on the popular 1.8-litre S model and came as either a three-door or a five-door. It featured 17-inch alloy wheels, privacy glass, air conditioning and a CD player, and cost £16,995 for the three-door or £18,495 for the five-door.

The Serengeti special edition arrived in early 2002. Looking closely, you can just see the special badge on the body ahead of the door mirror.

The Kalahari was based on the mid-range Freelander GS and came with 17-inch alloy wheels, leather-and-Alcantara seats, a CD autochanger and power-fold mirrors. Five-doors had an electric sunroof as standard, while the three-door had sunblinds and a hard loadspace cover. The Kalahari also featured two bright new colours – Borrego Yellow and Tangiers Orange. The latter was of course the colour used on the Land Rover models in the G4 Challenge event (see page 115). Three-door versions cost £18,795 and five-doors £19,995.

specification (but now only built to order) and the ES Premium remaining the top luxury model. However, the old GS and ES models were discontinued. In their place came the Serengeti and Kalahari, names already familiar as those of special-edition 1.8-litre petrol models (see sidebar).

The Td4 Serengeti was based on the S-specification model, with the addition of air conditioning, a single-slot CD player, 16-inch alloy wheels and privacy glass. The Td4 Kalahari was based on the old GS specification, with the addition of a CD autochanger, half-leather Alcantara upholstery and 17-inch Freedom alloys. Three-door Kalahari models also received sunblinds and a loadspace cover, while five-doors got power-fold mirrors and an electric sunroof.

Both models had special badging, and their badges were among the dealer-fitted items in the specification. The ES Premium continued to come with Alpaca leather seats and a Harmon Kardon ICE system, but Becker satnav, privacy glass and 17-inch Evolution alloy wheels were now all standard.

The Serengeti and Kalahari were priced at £1,000 over the S and GS models respectively. This represented approximately 70 per cent of the value of the additional specification, making the new models something of a bargain for buyers.

A glimpse of the future

It is impossible to say for certain whether the Freelander might have been replaced earlier if BMW had not sold Land Rover to Ford in 2000. Certainly, the industry norm for a vehicle like the Freelander, with high fashion appeal and a youthful image, would suggest that it might have been replaced no later than 2005, after a production run of around seven years.

Unconfirmed information from industry insiders has suggested that BMW's thinking about a second-generation Freelander involved the Land Rover model sharing mechanical elements with the German company's own X3 model. Whether that was true or not, the handover to Ford ownership meant that any plans BMW had been working on were scrapped. Ford had to start again.

Further insider information insists that a new provisional plan for the second-generation Freelander was in place during 2002, but that this had been abandoned by the end of the year. So Land Rover left themselves a tight three-year schedule to get the new Freelander into production in time for a launch provisionally scheduled for the first quarter of 2006. It

was said that plans to allow the new model to share componentry with the forthcoming Ford Focus and Volvo XC50 would make that tight deadline achievable.

However, one thing was already certain by the middle of 2003. This was that the second-generation Freelander would not be built at Land Rover's traditional Solihull home, but at the Halewood plant on Merseyside where Jaguar was already building its entry-level X-type saloon.

This news was released in mid-July, just a couple of weeks before Land Rover lifted the embargo on information about the heavily-revised 2004-model Freelanders. The official reason for the change of manufacturing venue was that it would reduce complexity at the Solihull site, where a fifth Land Rover line – for the

The ES Premium was a 2002 model, and carried HSE badges outside the UK. There were special badges and, of course, a top-quality two-tone leather interior.

VIN CODES FOR FREELANDERS, 2002–2004 (EXCEPT NAS MODELS)

The VIN codes used in this period consisted of 17 characters, made up of an 11-character prefix code and a six-digit serial number.

Example: SALLNAAA72A-123456.

This breaks down as follows:

SAL   Manufacturer code (Rover Group)

LN   Freelander

A   Standard trim

B = Commercial trim

A   Three-door body (Hardback or Softback)

    B = Five-door body (Station Wagon)

A   1.8-litre K-series petrol engine (HOU spec)

    B = 2.0-litre L-series diesel engine

    C = 1.8-litre K-series petrol engine (LOU spec)

    D = 1.8-litre K-series petrol engine (LOL spec)

    E = 2.0-litre Td4 diesel engine

    F = 1.8-litre K-series petrol engine (HOL spec)

    G = 2.5-litre V6 petrol engine (for unleaded fuel)

    H = 2.5-litre V6 petrol engine (for leaded fuel)

    J = 2.5-litre V6 petrol engine (for ethanol fuel)

1   RHD with 5-speed Steptronic (CommandShift) automatic gearbox

    2 = LHD with 5-speed Steptronic (CommandShift) automatic gearbox

7   RHD with 5-speed manual gearbox

    8 = LHD with 5-speed manual gearbox

2   Model-year 2002

    3 = 2003

    4 = 2004

A   Assembled at Solihull

    F = Shipped as KD for assembly in Thailand

    V = Shipped as KD for assembly in South Africa

123456 Serial number

Note: HOL spec is for High-octane leaded fuel

      HOU spec is for High-octane unleaded fuel

      LOL spec is for Low-octane leaded fuel

      LOU spec is for Low-octane unleaded fuel

Range Rover Sport which would compete with BMW's X5 and the new Porsche Cayenne – was about to be installed. And there certainly was no doubt that the Solihull plant was already becoming overcrowded.

Jaguar, of course, was another British marque which had been bought by Ford and figured alongside Land Rover in the American parent company's Premier Automotive Group. The two marques had in fact been getting increasingly close in recent months, not least through the appointment of Land Rover's Bob Dover as Chairman of both companies. Not yet officially announced were some important synergies between them: the next-generation Discovery was expected to feature at least one Jaguar engine, as were the new Range Rover Sport and other forthcoming Land Rover models.

The Halewood plant had once produced Ford Escorts, but was completely renovated in a £300 million scheme and re-opened as a Jaguar assembly plant in spring 2001. Production of the next-generation Freelander is expected to begin there towards the end of 2005.

The 2004 models

Increasingly under pressure from new rivals – the recent Nissan X-Trail being a very strong contender – Land Rover meanwhile had to make sure that the Freelander retained its market position for a further period of between two-and-a-half and three years. So the strategy began with a major package of changes for the 2004 models.

These were announced on August 1, 2003, with the first public viewing to be at the Frankfurt Motor Show in September and sales scheduled to begin in November. They had been developed under the code-name of L314 – the L standing for Land Rover but 314 simply being part of a Ford number sequence.

The changes overseen by Chief Programme Engineer Steve Routly included a new interior and a new face and tail. There was also an additional derivative, the Freelander Sport, which Land Rover touted as its sharpest-handling and sportiest production model ever.

The styling enhancements were carried out by a team led by Richard Woolley, working under Land Rover's Styling Director, Geoff Upex. The front bumper, headlamps and front grille were brand new, and adopted the distinctive family face pioneered by the third-generation Range Rover. The new, twin-pocket, clear lens headlamps were similar to those of the Freelander's big brother, and provided a higher light intensity – improved by 70 per cent. The bumpers were restyled and were now body-coloured.

At the rear, the bumper and lights were again new. The bumper was body-coloured, and tail lamps had been repositioned higher on it, making them easier to see and reducing the chance of them being obscured by road grime or mud and dust from off-road use.

There was also a comprehensive interior makeover, intended to improve comfort and the feeling of luxury. Most obvious was a new fascia, clearly inspired by the latest Range Rover and embodying the strong vertical

Above: The 2004-model instruments were not as easy to read as earlier types, and borrowed their style from the latest Range Rover.

Right: The 2004 models also had revised tail lights and new badging.

Below: The 2004 models had new front-end details, which freshened their appearance and gave them a family resemblance to the latest Range Rover and Discovery models.

The Sport model featured lowered suspension, and was claimed to have the best on-road handling of any Land Rover yet.

elements which had helped to make the interior styling of Land Rover's flagship model such a great success. New instruments and new switchgear also reflected Range Rover inspiration, with the dials standing proud of their background, and their bright rims giving them a sporty appearance.

The dashboard was also revised for 2004, picking up some themes from the latest Range Rover. This picture shows a RHD five-door model with the CommandShift automatic transmission.

New door trims on Station Wagons had a stronger horizontal emphasis, and all models now had the previous year's 'Premium' seats that offered better body and under-thigh comfort. There were also new upholstery fabrics, with a better quality 'feel' to them which matched the 2004 Freelander's more up-market pretensions.

On the mechanical side, the 1.8-litre petrol engine remained the entry-level option, while the Td4 diesel was expected to consolidate its position as the best-seller and the core of the range. The V6 of course remained available for flagship models. Both five-speed manual and five-speed automatic (CommandShift) gearboxes were improved for the facelifted model.

Perhaps most indicative of Land Rover's response to rivals in the Freelander's market sector, however, was the new Freelander Sport. Available for European markets only – where Land Rover was having to fight very hard to fend off the competition – this was available in either three-door or five-door form. To meet market demand for bigger and bigger wheels, this became the first Freelander to be factory fitted with 18-inch alloys, which were coupled to a lowered and firmer suspension, reducing roll and improving driver feedback. The result was more responsive driving behaviour on tarmac, and on smooth dirt or gravel roads – although the Sport models were clearly not intended to make heavy use of the Freelander's off-road abilities.

COLOURS AND TRIMS

2002 model-year (September 2001 to August 2002)

A range of 12 paint finishes was offered for the 2002 model-year. New colours Vienna Green and Zambezi Silver replaced Kent Green and Blenheim Silver, while Kinversand Bronze was dropped. There were two solid and three metallic colours, the remaining seven being micatallics.

In addition to the standard range of colours available throughout the season, Biarritz Blue was offered on the ESX models in the UK (see page 82).

Interior trim was rationalised again. There were now only two basic colours – Smokestone and new black. As before, certain interior trim combinations were 'recommended' (i.e. standard) although the alternative interior colour was mostly available to special order.

Three-door models had Jungle and TRek fabric as standard, while five-doors had new Canvas and Marl fabric. Leather was optional on all models. On three-doors the centre panels on leather seats were in Gunmetal, contrasting with Black or Smokestone outer panels. On five-doors, leather came in a combination of Light and Dark Smokestone or black and Dark Smokestone.

The combinations were as follows:

Alveston Red (micatallic)	Black
Bonatti Grey (metallic)	Black or Smokestone
Chawton White (solid)	Black or Smokestone
Epsom Green (micatallic)	Black or Smokestone
Icelandic Blue (micatallic)	Black
Java Black (micatallic)	Black or Smokestone
Monte Carlo Blue (micatallic)	Black
Oslo Blue (micatallic)	Black or Smokestone
Rutland Red (solid)	Black (Kingdom and Smokestone leather not available on 3-dr)
Vienna Green (micatallic)	Black or Smokestone
White Gold (metallic)	Black or Smokestone
Zambezi Silver (metallic)	Black or Smokestone

2003 model-year (September 2002 to October 2003)

The main range of paint finishes and interior options for 2003 was unchanged from the 2002 range. However, two new colours were available on limited-edition models in the UK, and a new interior option was available on top-model five-door Station Wagons (ES Premium models in the UK; HSE Models elsewhere).

The new paint colours were:
Borrego Yellow
Tangiers Orange
The new interior option was:
Black and Alpaca Beige leather

2004 model-year (November 2003 on)

There were 13 paint finishes for 2004. Icelandic Blue and White Gold were replaced by Helsinki Blue and Maya Gold, and Giverny Green was added; this left two solid colours, four metallics and seven micatallics.

There were now three interior colours – Black, Tundra and Alpaca – and four upholstery types – "Mogul technical fabric" (textured PVC, available only in Black), cloth, alcantara and leather. The cloth on five-door models was Jungle or Dune, and on five-doors was Mistral. On three-door models, all types of upholstery were available in Black; Tundra could be had only in Dune cloth, alcantara or leather; and Alpaca was a leather-only option. On five-doors, Black was again available for all upholstery types, while Tundra and Alpaca were both available in cloth, alcantara or leather.

Certain paint and interior colour combinations were highly recommended ('Designer's Choice', or 1 in the table below), others were 'recommended' (2) and yet others 'available' (3). Tundra was not available with some paint colours, as indicated.

	Black	Tundra	Alpaca
Alveston Red (micatallic)	2	3	2
Bonatti Grey (metallic)	2	2	2
Chawton White (solid)	2	2	3
Epsom Green (metallic)	2	2	1
Giverny Green (micatallic)	2	N/A	1
Helsinki Blue (metallic)	2	N/A	3
Java Black (micatallic)	2	2	1
Maya Gold (metallic)	2	3	1
Monte Carlo Blue (micatallic)	2	N/A	3
Oslo Blue (micatallic)	3	N/A	2
Rutland Red (solid)	2	N/A	3
Vienna Green (micatallic)	2	1	3
Zambezi Silver (micatallic)	1	3	2

Chapter Seven

New frontiers

The North American Freelander

Although Land Rovers were first exported to the USA and Canada in 1949, they did not sell in large quantities. The vastness of the territory made it hard for the old Rover Company – which was then a small independent motor manufacturer – to establish enough dealerships to cover the area properly. In addition, it was an uphill struggle to take sales away from the established and respected domestic 4x4 marque, Jeep.

Although Land Rovers remained available in both the USA and Canada throughout the 1950s and 1960s, sales were slow. When the later 1960s brought a wave of new vehicle-related legislation in North America, Rover tried hard to make its 4x4s comply, but the cost of alterations was never fully justified by the expected sales. Exhaust emissions legislation proved the biggest problem, as emissions control equipment took power away from engines which did not have a lot of it in the first place. First, the long-wheelbase Land Rovers disappeared from North America in 1967. Then, by 1974, legislation had become so tough that Rover (by now part of the ailing British Leyland combine) could no longer justify the cost of keeping the short-wheelbase models compliant, and pulled out of the market altogether.

The Solihull 4x4s returned in 1987, although in the shape of the Range Rover rather than under the Land Rover name. The collapse of sales in Africa and some other traditional Land Rover markets in the developing world had forced the company to look elsewhere for sales, and its MD in the mid-1980s, Tony Gilroy, decided to focus on developed countries in Continental Europe and North America.

Range Rover of North America (as the US company was initially called) created its own niche market for a luxury 4x4, filled it admirably with the Range Rover, and then went on to import the Defender from 1992 and the Discovery from 1994. With the arrival of the Defender, the company was re-named Land Rover North America (LRNA), and it still had this name when the Freelander was launched in the USA and Canada in 2001.

The North American launch

Land Rover planned the Freelander's North American launch very carefully indeed. Not only did the product have to be right, but the pre-launch marketing and awareness-building campaign had to be right on target. For, although Land Rover was a major player in many territories around the world, it was still a small niche-market manufacturer as far as North America was concerned.

The stakes were high. If all went according to plan, Freelander sales in North America would more than

DID YOU KNOW?
www.freelander.com

Early on in the North American pre-launch campaign, the company established an internet web site as a 'teaser' for North American customers. The first of its kind in the motor industry, www.freelander.com was an interactive programme which gave customers the opportunity to sign up and become one of the first Freelander owners in North America. It also offered a behind-the-scenes look through the Flash animated introduction that demonstrated the versatility and advanced features of the vehicle as well as the authentic British heritage of Land Rover.

The site was designed and managed by New York-based AGENCY.COM, the company which had been responsible for the official Land Rover North America web site since June 2000.

Land Rover North America was delighted with the web site's success. Not only did it spread the word about the Freelander, but it also generated 618 confirmed orders and 1027 additional sales leads before the new model went on sale.

The Freelander was introduced to the North American press at a launch event in Iceland. Clearly visible here are the running lights in the bumper moulding wraparounds, as demanded by North American regulations.

double the marque's sales across the Atlantic to around 50,000 vehicles a year. This would immediately make North America into Land Rover's most important overseas market – a far cry from the early 1970s when most Land Rovers sold to developing countries and North America was an also-ran. In addition, if these Freelanders inspired enthusiasm for the brand, there would be a long-term effect on overall Land Rover sales, as first-time Freelander owners traded up for a Discovery or a Range Rover.

A major campaign to arouse customer interest in the USA and Canada was begun many months before the vehicles actually went on sale there, and one result of this was that potential customers in those countries had some sneak previews of the 2002-specification models before anyone else. The pre-launch campaign embraced a dedicated web site (see sidebar), a ride-and-drive exercise for the motoring media in Canada during March 2001, plus a second one in Iceland that autumn, and a slick dealer launch called Sands of Adventure at Lake Las Vegas in Nevada. The choice of a North American Specification (NAS) Freelander for the

three-millionth Land Rover celebration (see Chapter Six) was also designed to gather publicity in North America, while emphasising elsewhere the importance which Land Rover attached to this market.

There were further 'teases' too: specially-prepared concept versions of the Freelander, known as the Kensington and Kalahari (see sidebar), were displayed at the Detroit Motor Show in January 2001 and at the New York Auto Show in April. Then, just as the Freelander was about to reach showrooms at the end of the year, a supercharged concept vehicle by Callaway (see sidebar), designed to arouse more interest and generate more media publicity, was displayed at the SEMA tuning and performance show.

From the start, the intention had been to market the North American Freelander initially only in five-door Station Wagon form with the V6 engine and Steptronic

All NAS Freelanders had the Steptronic automatic transmission, which was renamed the CommandShift transmission at about the time the vehicles went on sale in North America.

All North American Freelanders were powered by the 2.5-litre V6 engine. The longer nose of V6 models is quite apparent in this picture of an HSE at speed.

automatic transmission – which in practice was rebranded as the CommandShift transmission when the model was launched. However, a three-door V6 was present at the Canadian ride-and-drive exercise in March 2001, and as early as November 2000, Bill Baker of LRNA's public relations department was happy to admit that the company was considering marketing a limited-edition three-door model later on as a sporty niche-market variant.

In fact, the three-door would reach North America as a 2003 model, slightly under a year after the original five-door Station Wagon had gone on sale. After the concept vehicles had been seen at the New York Auto Show in April 2001, a spokesman for LRNA also said that the company was 'reviewing the possibility' of bringing the 1.8-litre model into North America. At the time of writing, however, that possibility had not become a reality.

A great deal of information had been carefully 'leaked' about the North American Freelander before it went on sale, not least to counter negative stories about specifications based on knowledge of the older European models. One of those 'leaked' stories concerned the cupholders – which were then very important items of

equipment on North American vehicles because of the habit in that country of buying a large drink at a fast-food outlet in mid-journey and drinking it while on the move. As Land Rover's chief, Bob Dover joked to the media at an early briefing, the cupholders were being redesigned to suit American-size cups – which were often larger than those used in Europe. Quite obviously, the North American models were also going to have side running lights, and the locations of these in the front and rear bumper wraparounds became clear when the Freelander was shown for the first time at the 2001 Detroit Motor Show. The Detroit show Freelanders also dispensed with the roof-mounted aerial of European models, relying instead on an antenna mounted in the body glass.

The 2002 NAS Freelanders actually went on sale at the very end of November 2001 in some areas of the country, although the official on-sale date was the beginning of December. They were well-appointed, and even the base model came with electric front windows and a heated windscreen as standard. There were three specification levels, called S, SE and HSE. The entry-level Freelander S had cloth upholstery, 16-inch alloy wheels on 215/65 R 16 tyres, and an AM/FM audio system with in-dash CD player. Moving up to the SE

The interior of the more expensive NAS Freelanders featured leather upholstery.

Reassurance for North American buyers came in the form of pictures of a Freelander cutaway, which revealed the side-impact bars in the doors, and other safety features.

brought leather upholstery and steering-wheel trim, remote controls for the audio system on the steering wheel, 17-inch alloy wheels with 225/55 R 17 tyres, Optikool privacy glass behind the B-pillars, twin illuminated visor vanity mirrors, a roller blind rear cargo cover, and roof rails.

The top-model HSE offered a Harman Kardon high-output audio system with a six-disc CD changer, a Becker voice-command navigation system, an electric sunroof, Alpaca Beige leather upholstery with a more conventional lateral stitch pattern, and 17-inch flat-spoke alloy wheels.

As options, there were heated front seats for all models, while the S and SE could both be fitted with the top-spec audio system and six-disc CD changer. The SE could have an electric sunroof, although S buyers were denied this option. There were 11 exterior colours available on the mid-range SE models, but only six for the S and a different six for the HSE (see sidebar).

Land Rover North America made bullish suggestions about sales of 20,000 Freelanders in 2002, but the reality was rather different. Even though the vehicle was very well-received by the North American motoring media, in its first 12 months on sale (November 2001 to November 2002) it actually attracted just over 14,000 buyers. The main reason was that the competition was getting more intense: during 2002, the Freelander was battling against the excellent new Nissan X-Trail and the Honda Pilot, as well as the Ford Escape.

The SE3 and the 2003 models

The promised three-door Freelander arrived for the 2003 model-year in North America, under the name of SE3. It was expected to give a boost to sales and, in particular, to attract buyers in sunny, 'open-air' states such as California and Florida. Its 'fun' image was reinforced by the choice of just five bright exterior colours.

The Freelander SE3 did not differ in its essentials from the three-door models familiar in other countries where the Freelander was sold. However, its

The three-door Freelander arrived as a 2003 model and was badged as an SE3. Note how the Borrego Yellow paint on this model has not been carried over to the air intake panel in the front apron.

Opposite: In this configuration, the Freelander seemed ideally suited to the great American outdoors.

An all-black interior added to the impact of the **SE3** model.

The removable targa roofs of the SE3 could be stowed in a zipped bag behind the seats – just as they always had been on three-door Freelanders for other markets.

configuration for North America was very specific. The V6 engine with CommandShift transmission was of course the only powertrain available, while 17-inch three-spoke wheels (the Evolution type) with 225/55 mud-and-snow tyres were standard wear. As on all North American Freelanders, ABS was standard and brought with it EBD, HDC and ETC.

The SE3 came in Hardback form, no Softback alternative being offered. The Hardback windows and the fixed side glass were all in black-tinted 'privacy' glass, and a front A-frame brush bar and roof rails were also part of the standard specification. Air conditioning, cruise control and a heated windscreen were also standard.

All SE3s had a 60–40 split rear bench seat, and their seats were upholstered in black 'Technical Fabric' vinyl unless buyers ordered the extra-cost heated black or beige leather seats. A leather-trimmed steering wheel was fitted with both vinyl and leather upholstery, and a 240-watt Harman Kardon ICE with in-dash single-CD player was standard, a six-CD stacker being another extra-cost option. Like three-door models for other markets, the North American SE3 came with a detachable, roof-mounted radio antenna.

There were changes to the five-door models for 2003, too. These had the larger 64-litre (16.9 US gallons) fuel tank and the quieter and more efficient heating-ventilating-air conditioning system. Body side mouldings were also standardised to protect the vehicle's flanks. Once again, the three trim levels of S, SE and HSE were available, while the exterior and interior colour choices remained the same.

DID YOU KNOW?
LRNA becomes AMJLRNA

After Ford bought Land Rover in 2000, the company was allocated to its Premier Automotive Group (PAG) and over the next two years or so a number of administrative changes were put into effect.

As part of these, Land Rover North America ceased to exist and was absorbed into a new administrative division which embraced all the British marques within the PAG. This new division, which was established early in 2002, was known by the cumbersome title of Aston Martin Jaguar Land Rover North America, or AMJLRNA for short. The Land Rover administrative headquarters was moved from its premises at Lanham, Maryland to join the Jaguar and Aston Martin components in Irvine, California.

NORTH AMERICAN CONCEPTS (1): THE KENSINGTON AND KALAHARI

In the early months of 2001, Land Rover North America showed two concept versions of the Freelander at motor shows. Prepared by Land Rover Special Vehicles, and known as the Kensington and the Kalahari, these were designed to show off the two contrasting extremes of the Freelander's personality. At the one extreme, the Kensington was the smart and luxurious urban commuter vehicle, while at the other, the Kalahari was the rugged off-roader designed for a life of adventure. Both, of course, were left-hand drive V6 models.

The Kensington was finished in Black Cherry and featured colour-coded bumpers, door mirrors and exterior trim in the style planned for Autobiography vehicles. The front apron insert, normally finished in the body colour, was painted in a contrasting Titanium Silver, exactly as on the Freelander Autobiography at the 2000 British International Motor Show. The same colour was used on the special 18-inch Comet alloy wheels, which borrowed their style from the similarly named wheels available for Range Rovers.

The interior featured remodelled seats in tan leather with saddle-style stitching. The entire dashboard and the lower door panels were in black, with tan leather gaiters for the gear lever and handbrake with tan upper door panel sections. Deep-pile carpets and a premium ICE system gave a hint of the luxury items which would later be made available, as did the leather-rimmed steering wheel in two-tone black and tan.

The Kalahari was finished in Molten Orange, the colour used for the dealer-competition TReK vehicles,

The Kensington's all-black dash prefigured the 2002 NAS models..

with a matt black bonnet. All the exterior plastic trim was refinished in semi-matt black, and one protection plate had been added over the steering and sump, with a second over the rear exhaust silencer. A heavy-duty receiver hitch at the rear was matched by a tough A-frame with recovery points at the front, each designed to accept a demountable winch. On the roof was a full-length heavy-duty roof rack, and above the windscreen was mounted a Camel Trophy-style light pod with four Safari 1000 lights. Extra floodlights were mounted to the roof at the rear. The tyres were custom-made off-road types on 17-inch Freedom alloy wheels.

Inside, the Kalahari boasted grey leather seats with Active Canvas fabric inserts and orange piping. The door trims and dash were black. Further orange piping was used on the gearshift knob and handbrake lever, and the radio panel was replaced by a row of switches for the roof-mounted lights.

There were hints of the Camel Trophy and TReK in the Kalahari.

To promote the Freelander's arrival, Land Rover North America commissioned Callaway Cars to produce this striking high-performance Freelander concept vehicle.

NORTH AMERICAN CONCEPTS (2): THE CALLAWAY SUPERCHARGED FREELANDER

While the Kensington and Kalahari show vehicles demonstrated the two extremes of the Freelander's character to potential customers in North America, LRNA also decided to capitalise on the vehicle's performance potential. So they got together with respected high-performance experts Callaway to produce a third show special.

Callaway was a natural choice for the job. Their reputation in the high-performance world had already led to one successful collaboration with LRNA, when the company had designed a limited-edition high-performance Range Rover, sold only in North America during 1999. So a deal was done for the company to prepare a high-performance Freelander concept vehicle in time for the SEMA tuning show in Las Vegas which opened on 30 October 2001.

With little time to get the job done, LRNA could not obtain a North American specification Freelander for Callaway to work on. However, they did manage to get their hands on a redundant concept vehicle from the UK – the five-door Freelander Autobiography (SALLNABG11A-584387) which had been displayed at the 2000 British International Motor Show. As this already had a number of cosmetic enhancements, the finished product was going to be that much more spectacular. The only drawback (which few people even seemed to notice) was that it had right-hand drive.

The vehicle reached Callaway's premises in Old Lyme, Connecticut in the late autumn of 2001, leaving the company just over six weeks to create a show special. The brief was to develop a spectacular high-performance Freelander, with the bias clearly being towards on-road rather than off-road use.

The result was a visual stunner, with a road presence which the standard Freelander undoubtedly lacked. The original Azul Blue paintwork and the metallic silver grille bar, and the idea of a matching apron insert were retained, but the exterior was given a make-over by Paul Deutschmann, a Montreal designer who had collaborated with Callaway on several projects. It featured a new front apron with integral aerodynamic splitter to give greater downforce at high speed, plus a metallic silver skid plate.

Aerodynamic sill panels were styled to resemble extruded metal beams and were said to improve high-speed stability. Wheel flaps served as mudguards when mounted at the rear of the wheel openings but as air deflectors when fitted to the front, forcing air around the tyres and so reducing high-speed drag. Final touches were an air diffuser lip on the rear apron and a distinctive aluminium heat shield with exposed fasteners which echoed those on the wheels.

Those wheels were 18-inch two-piece lightweight alloys, featuring custom wheel hub pilots and a spoke design which allowed a clear view of the Callaway-branded brake callipers. Each one carried a Callaway centre cap, and Pirelli P-Zero 255/45R 18Z high-performance road tyres were fitted all round.

The big wheels created space for big brakes, enhanced to match the extra performance. Both front and rear discs were grooved and ventilated, the fronts measuring 332mm in diameter and 32mm in width, while the measurements of the rears were 304mm and 25mm respectively. The front discs received additional cooling air from carbon-fibre ducts in the front apron and the massive four-piston callipers were, like the discs, adapted from Callaway racing technology. Each disc wore a custom cover, anodised in Callaway blue to match the Azul Blue bodywork and to meet the contemporary fashion for having something stylish visible through the wheel spokes.

Suspension modifications included a full complement of Callaway Sport Tuned springs with higher spring rates and revalved dampers, as well as several custom-engineered and machined components such as a larger-diameter anti-roll bar. The low-profile tyres and suspension modifications left the Freelander sitting a full two inches lower than standard, once again demonstrating that the bias of this vehicle was towards on-road behaviour and away from off-road ability.

Key to the whole concept was of course the engine changes, which took the standard 2.5-litre V6 up from 177bhp to 250bhp with 260lb ft of torque at 4,000rpm and a power band which Callaway described as broad and user-friendly. Performance figures have not been independently confirmed, but 0–60mph was expected to take around 7.7 seconds; a standard V6 Freelander takes 10.1 seconds to hit 60mph from rest.

'Our engineering objective was to combine superior

Uprated brakes were of course an essential feature of the high-performance Callaway Freelander.

COLOURS AND TRIMS IN NORTH AMERICA

2002 model-year (December 2001 to August 2002)

A range of 11 paint finishes was offered for the 2002 model-year, but of these only six were available on the S models and a different six on the HSE.

Models with the entry-level S specification had fabric upholstery. SE models had leather upholstery with the seat stitching in familiar Freelander style, while the HSE models had leather upholstery with a more sober stitch pattern.

The combinations were as follows:

Exterior	Interior (S)	Interior (SE)	Interior (HSE)
Alveston Red	N/A	Smokestone Grey	N/A
Bonatti Grey	N/A	Ash Black and Alpaca Beige	N/A
Chawton White	Ash Black or Smokestone	Ash Black or Smokestone	Alpaca Beige with Black trim
Epsom Green	Ash Black	Ash Black or Ash Black with Alpaca Beige	Alpaca Beige with Black trim
Icelandic Blue	Ash Black	Ash Black or Ash Black with Alpaca Beige	N/A
Java Black	Ash Black or Smokestone	Ash Black or Ash Black with Alpaca Beige	Alpaca Beige with Black trim
Monte Carlo Blue	N/A	Ash Black or Smokestone	N/A
Oslo Blue	N/A	Ash Black or Ash Black with Alpaca Beige	Alpaca Beige with Black trim
Rutland Red	Ash Black	Ash Black or Ash Black with Alpaca Beige	N/A
White Gold	N/A	Ash Black or Ash Black with Alpaca Beige	Alpaca Beige with Black trim
Zambezi Silver	Smokestone Grey	Ash Black or Smokestone	Alpaca Beige with Black trim

2003 model-year (September 2002 on)

The same range of 11 paint finishes was offered for the 2003 model-year, but there was a different selection of just five colours available for the SE3 model. Of these, Java Black was available only at extra cost on both SE3 and five-door models.

SE3s came as standard with black Technical Fabric vinyl upholstery while all colours could be ordered optionally with Black leather or Alpaca Beige leather upholstery.

The five SE3 exterior colours were:

Borrego Yellow – Java Black – Monte Carlo Blue – Tangiers Orange – Zambezi Silver

2004 model-year

The 2004 model-year colour and trim combinations had not been announced at the time this book went to press.

The heart of the Callaway Freelander was a supercharged derivative of the V6 engine.

driveability with the flattest possible torque curve for the broadest range of high performance – all without sacrificing fuel economy,' explained Jim Jones, Callaway's engine development manager. To help meet this objective, the team at Callaway Advanced Technology decided to fit a supercharger.

This called for a specially designed aluminium inlet manifold, with an optimised inlet duct length to ensure consistently strong performance all the way from idle to 6,200rpm. In addition, the Callaway engineers developed an intercooler-heat exchanger system which was liquid-cooled by a high-capacity electric pump. A

Small details helped to make the Callaway what it was; these are the exhaust tailpipes.

new throttle housing had been CNC machined from an aluminium billet and featured dual throttle ports and integral idle air control. The finishing touch was a carbon fibre engine cover which wrapped around the supercharger and, of course, carried the Callaway name.

As on the Range Rover in 1999, the exhaust system also came in for attention. To gain equal power distribution to the twin outlet pipes, the entire system was repositioned and modified. The new exhaust included a stainless steel silencer and stainless steel exhaust tips, tuned to give a satisfying resonance.

VIN CODES FOR NAS FREELANDERS

The VIN codes used on North American models in this period consisted of 17 characters, made up of an 11-character prefix code and a six-digit serial number.

Example: SALNY22202A-123456.

This breaks down as follows:

SAL Manufacturer code (Land Rover)

NY Freelander

2 Four-door body (i.e. Station Wagon)

    3 = Three-door body (SE3)

2 2.5-litre V6 petrol engine

2 5-speed CommandShift automatic gearbox

0 Security check digit

    (0 to 9, or X)

2 Model-year 2002

    3 = 2003

A Assembled at Solihull

123456 Serial number

Chapter Eight

What's it like to drive?

What the press thought

The first time I drove a Freelander was in Spain, on the relatively uncrowded roads of the Sierra Blanca, near Las Dunas on the coast. I'd been invited to the international press ride-and-drive exercise which was held in mid-November 1997, far enough in advance of the first showroom sales to give all the journalists

The standard five-speed manual box has always been quite slick and easy to use – not at all the way many people imagine Land Rover gearboxes to be!

plenty of time to record their impressions in print and whet the appetites of potential buyers.

To be honest, I wasn't quite sure what to expect. I had a feeling that this new Land Rover was going to be very different from the marque's traditional products, and I had a few misgivings about whether it would live up to the abilities I associated with the Land Rover name.

The vehicles on offer at that press launch were all from the R... BAC batch of early production examples, and there was a choice of 1.8-litre petrol or 2.0-litre L-series diesel engines. All the gearboxes were five-speed manuals, of course.

I forget now whether it was a petrol or a diesel Freelander that I drove first, but I do remember experiencing some very mixed reactions. It didn't feel like a traditional Land Rover at all; the controls were light, the engine revved freely, and it seemed to accelerate pretty well.

On the road, I remember being a little disappointed. The whole thing felt very much like a small modern car, with similar levels of mechanical noise, a similar ride from its all-independent suspension, and much sharper and more car-like steering than any Land Rover I'd ever driven before.

That, of course, was the whole point of the Freelander. In its on-road behaviour, it had been designed to make the step into Land Rover ownership easy for those who had been used to conventional cars. There was none of the apparent bulkiness and weight of a traditional 4x4, and nothing which would make a driver new to the vehicle feel uneasy. Yet it retained enough design cues to make anyone familiar with vehicles like the Discovery and Range Rover feel that this could just about be an offspring of the same stable.

However – and I have to be absolutely honest about this – it was the visual design cues which made the

Freelander feel like a Land Rover. Everything else about it immediately shouted 'modern small car'. It didn't drive like a Land Rover at all, and in that respect I thought – and I still think – that it lacked some of the essential character of Solihull's traditional 4x4 products.

We did, though, get a chance to try it out on a fairly undemanding off-road route through the Sierra Blanca – a route which had been carefully selected to illustrate the Freelander's off-road strengths and not to show up its weaknesses. Realistically, this was exactly the sort of terrain which most Freelander buyers were likely to think was quite extreme. Our route included a few opportunities to try out the Hill Descent Control on steep downhill gravel tracks, and the vehicle generally performed well – certainly in a way which would impress anyone used to a conventional small car.

The ride-and-drive exercise gave us the opportunity to try different varieties, and I swapped from petrol to diesel model (or was it the other way round?) at the mid-day lunch stop. We were able, too, to compare the youthful three-door model with the alternative family-orientated five-door.

The overall layout of the controls is very car-like, although the weighting of the controls and their more solid feel are factors which reinforce the factor of Land Rover heritage.

A Freelander Station Wagon on the picturesque roads in the Beaujolais region of France, where the 2001 models were introduced to the international media.

Country roads in the Beaujolais region again . . . the Freelander's behaviour on such roads is similar to that of a small-to-medium car.

It is interesting, I think, that I came away from that event in Spain with a distinct preference for the diesel engine. On paper, it didn't give the acceleration of the petrol engine, but on the road it didn't feel that much slower. What it did do was to feel much more like a traditional Land Rover engine, with more noticeable low-down torque and less willingness to accelerate hard at higher speeds. A few weeks before the Freelander event, I'd had a press loan of a Rover 620 SLDi with the L-series diesel engine, so that I would be able to make comparisons when I drove the diesel Freelander. I'd liked the engine a lot in that Rover, and I was pleased to discover that the Freelander installation wasn't much noisier (although there was a difference) and wasn't very noticeably less accelerative (though, again, there was a difference).

The 1.8-litre petrol engine didn't appeal to me very much. It made the Freelander feel too much like an ordinary car, with good acceleration at high speeds and not a lot of torque down low – which made for more frequent gearchanging if you wanted to make swift progress. Somehow, it sounded buzzy, too. I realised that this was a product of its multi-valve configuration and that this and its ability to rev high would be familiar to anyone transferring to the Freelander from an ordinary car. But it wasn't for me.

It was interesting to compare the interior treatments of the three-door and five-door models. I'd already seen them at the technical seminar back in June that year, but there's nothing like driving a vehicle to get a proper feel for its interior ambience. The dashboard and control layout was the same in both models, of course, and it seemed pleasantly chunky with reassuring echoes of the fascia used in early Discovery models – plus the rather unfortunate retention of the Discovery's bright blue plastic, which I never had liked much! What I did believe was a serious omission was an inboard armrest for the driver; perhaps it came from too many years of driving a Range Rover, but it definitely felt as if something was missing.

Seat fabrics were different between the two models, but I found the differences between the shapes of the fabric seat panels too subtle to register. Much more noticeable was the fact that there were vast acres of painted metal inside the three-door model, while in the five-door they were all hidden behind neat and sober trim panels. Those swathes of metal certainly could be seen as a reminder of the rather spartan interior of early Land Rover utilities, but I wondered whether the young buyers in the three-door's target audience might expect something a little less basic. I was particularly concerned about the angled pillar behind the door on each side of the three-door; it seemed to me that it not only blocked the view out for rear seat passengers, but also gave them a pretty unappetising panel of painted metal to look at.

Comparing the three-door with the five-door body wasn't so easy, though. There was no doubt that the three-door looked more striking, especially with the roof off, while the five-door was very definitely more sober in appearance despite the slightly quirky Discovery-derived stepped roofline.

Nevertheless, I came away with a very firm preference for the five-door Station Wagon. This was probably because I saw it as an altogether more practical vehicle for everyday use than the three-door. If you're going to carry passengers regularly, you really need two doors on each side of your car; one just isn't enough. As for the delights of open-air motoring with the soft top off, I reckoned it was fine out there in sunny Spain, but not something which would happen very often back home in Britain where it rains even when the sun comes out!

So much for what I thought – but those were just one man's opinions. What did the rest of the motoring press think of the new Freelander?

The first Freelanders

The announcement of the Freelander at the end of 1997 was widely viewed as a major event by the motoring media, and the motoring magazines fell over one another to get an example on long-term loan and to put forward their opinions. Most of those opinions, in the English-language magazines at least, were very positive.

Rather than fill this chapter with a tedious series of quotations which all more or less say the same thing, I've

All Freelanders have a relatively small luggage area behind the rear seats. It is tall rather than deep, however, and will hold more than seems likely at first sight.

decided to look at representative press evaluations which were written when the vehicles were new. So for the very first Freelanders, I've chosen to focus on a feature in *What Car?* magazine for February 1998 which evaluated a 1.8-litre petrol Station Wagon, and on a pair of features in *Car* magazine for December 1997, which evaluated a Station Wagon with the L-series diesel engine.

All the early road test vehicles were from the batch of Freelanders registered in the R... BAC series and were early production examples. The Station Wagons were early enough to have blacked-out door window frames (see Chapter Three). *What Car?* seems to have had access to at least three vehicles (R201 BAC, R202 BAC and R208 BAC), while *Car* evaluated R208 BAC.

The *Car* magazine view

Car magazine ran two concurrent features on the Freelander, the first (by John Simister) recording impressions of R208 BAC on a long trans-European drive, and the second (by Paul Horrell) comparing it with two direct rivals in the shape of the Jeep Cherokee and the five-door Toyota RAV4.

The Freelander came out well in the comparison, and Horrell concluded that 'for people . . . looking for a roomy, civilised road car that's also tall and chunky, and can hold its own in light off-roading, the Freelander will fit the bill.' On the road, it was impressive. Simister wrote: 'There's none of the topply, top-heavy, trip-over feel you'll find in some 4x4s. Instead, the steering is precise and progressive, the body leans little, and the Freelander tracks through a corner with barely a hint of a trajectory-widening tendency. In short, it handles like a proper car, and rides like one too.'

Horrell reinforced the message. He argued that, compared with the RAV4, the Freelander's steering 'has a more remote feel about it, but it's very able: there's more grip, less understeer, and generally it makes more serene progress. Mid-corner bumps don't bother it at all. There's little roll, partly because the engine is mounted low in the body to keep the centre of gravity down. The steering's well geared and accurate, and it's stable under its brakes.'

The diesel engine, though, received lukewarm praise. 'As the rev ceiling approaches,' wrote John Simister, 'the power tails right off, which is as you'd expect in a diesel but you encounter it more because the Freelander is quite short-geared. Off-roadability is why, of course, but in return you'd expect stonking pull at low engine speeds in the higher gears, just as you get in more car-shaped Rovers fitted with this engine. It never quite materialises, though, not least because the Freelander five-door weighs a hefty 1,525kg [3,363lb] . . . Still, this is a smooth and refined engine as DI diesels go, and it doesn't wake the dead when starting from cold.' Nevertheless, it did have 'a pervasive background drone on the cruise.'

Paul Horrell generally shared Simister's view of the engine: 'If the Freelander's diesel engine has to work hard, it's agreeable enough while it's at it: the 2.0-litre L-series has a broad rev range and the gearbox is well oiled.' Ultimately, though, while 'the Freelander is an easy thing to drive . . . it'll never be rewarding in the pure driving sense.'

The *What Car?* view

What Car? didn't pull any punches in their evaluation of the Freelander, giving it their Car of the Year and Off-Roader of the Year awards simultaneously. 'Once the word has got around that there's an off-roader that dispenses with the dynamics of a truck and carries a Land Rover badge, there'll be no stopping it,' they said. 'What really impresses is the way it lets you have it all – an image of aristocratic hauteur and a build of proletarian honesty packed into the one charismatic frame.'

On the whole, the *What Car?* team rather liked the 1.8-litre petrol engine. 'The Freelander works well from 2,750rpm, so it isn't essential to hang onto the intermediate gears when overtaking. Which is just as well,' they argued, 'because its engine gets boomy if pushed hard, but usually it's hardly noticeable. That's

especially true on the motorway where a leggy fifth makes it a quiet cruiser.' With an average of 33.3mpg during their test, the 1.8-litre Freelander proved encouragingly frugal, too – although the 6,000-mile service intervals were clearly going to push up the cost of ownership.

Nevertheless, the driving experience wasn't all good news. 'Comfort and refinement have been allowed to water down any element of sportiness . . . the price you pay for this compliant springing is the Freelander's tendency to allow a small degree of pitch and wallow over poorly surfaced roads taken at speed. You also have to put up with extra roll in the bends ... It can also feel sloppy if presented with a series of bends taken in quick succession.

'There's a deadness to the Freelander's steering in the first quarter of a turn, but after that it's direct, consistent and well weighted. You appreciate this characteristic if you do any off-roading as there's almost no kickback through the wheel, but it makes pedalling the car on quick, winding, undulating roads somewhat untidy.'

Interior appointments came in for praise, as did the space available. However, the driving position was considered to be less than perfect. 'Most people will be able to find the right driving position even though the steering wheel moves only one way, up and down. The seat also strikes the right blend of firmness and comfort; it's just a shame that the base isn't a little longer, and there's no height adjustment. As it is, you may feel a little too highly perched.' In the back, 'legroom, even for six-footers, is fine . . . (but) . . . some of the Land Rover's passenger space comes at the expense of cargo capacity . . . its boot is of the slim-and-tall variety.'

Lastly, *What Car?* made the point several times that £995 was a big price to pay for the difference between the entry-level di and the more comprehensively-equipped XEdi model, especially when it included some items which they thought should have been standard. 'Rover is far from generous when equipping its cars, and that mean streak seems to have rubbed off on Land Rover. . . . It's reasonable that air-con, alloy wheels and possibly an electric sunroof should be cost options on a base-trim model; but less forgivable that anti-lock brakes, a passenger airbag and seat-height adjustment . . . are withheld.'

The 2001 and later models

I was lucky enough to drive several more Freelanders

over the next few years, and in particular I asked Land Rover for a press loan of a petrol-engined three-door model to see if my initial reactions had been wrong. However, a week with R212 BAC didn't change my mind one little bit, smart though it was with its softback and gleaming black paint. If I were to have a Freelander, I decided, I'd want one with five doors and a solid roof, plus the more Land Rover-like feel that comes from the bottom-end torque of the diesel engine.

By the time the revised 2001 models were released in the autumn of 2000, Land Rover had passed from BMW ownership into membership of Ford's Premier Automotive Group. In wondering if the green Land Rover oval might eventually take on the blue background of the Ford oval, I suspect I wasn't alone among the journalists invited out to the ride-and-drive exercise in the wine-growing region near Bordeaux in France! But any changes injected by Ford were still a long way off, and in fact the new models said more about what BMW had done for the company than they did about what Ford might or might not do later.

The whole event was based on Bordeaux airport, where Land Rover had hired a large suite for the several weeks it took to give what seemed like half the world's motoring journalists a chance to try the new models. There was, as usual, a good mixed road route which included picturesque little villages and multi-lane motorways for high-speed work. The new models' off-road prowess was demonstrated in some more picturesque driving through traditional vineyards on hillsides. Then of course, Land Rover made sure that we didn't go away without a couple of bottles of the local produce to help us remember the event.

The 1.8-litre petrol engine was still going to be available, with a few minor changes to help it meet new emissions regulations and reduce servicing requirements. It came with a new gearbox, too. However, if there were any 1.8-litre models out there in France, I didn't see them. Land Rover's aim was to get us behind the wheel of the new 2.5-litre V6 and Td4 diesel models, to demonstrate the two new engines and the new Steptronic automatic transmission.

'The new Freelanders have suspension revisions, designed to improve the ride and handling, and they have more responsive power steering,' I wrote in the November 2000 issue of *LAND ROVER enthusiast*. However, 'to be honest, none of this was immediately obvious ... but it probably would be in a back-to-back comparison.' The interiors all seemed more sober than before (which I thought was a good thing), but I'd have

been hard pressed to explain exactly what was different about them. There was still no inboard driver's armrest, though – and I still felt the Freelander needed one.

Three-door and five-door bodies were unchanged – and you had to look really hard to spot the lengthened nose of the V6 Freelanders – but there had been some very welcome changes to the ABS installation. The new Teves system which replaced the original Bosch type turned out to be very much quieter in operation, particularly when it was powering the Hill Descent Control or the Electronic Traction Control.

I was expecting great things from the new V6 engine. With 177bhp and 177lb ft of torque, it promised a lot more than the 1.8-litre petrol engine, which I hadn't liked much. As I had done with the L-series diesel three years earlier, I arranged a press loan of a Rover saloon car (a 75) with the same engine shortly before the Freelander event in France. It impressed me enormously with both its refinement and its performance. Certainly, the automatic transmission and the extra weight of the Freelander were likely to blunt its edge, I thought, but I had the feeling that this would be the Freelander for me.

What I didn't quite expect was that the torque peak would be so high up the rev range. So, although there was enough torque at lower engine speeds to give reasonably swift acceleration, the engine made the Freelander feel even more like an ordinary car than before, with eager acceleration at motorway speeds. I'd hoped for the beefy low-down torque of the big American-born V8 engine which Land Rover had been using in its other models for 30 years – but it wasn't at all like that.

What I did like about the V6 was the noises it made. As I wrote in that appraisal for *LAND ROVER enthusiast*

Is the Td4 common-rail diesel engine the best engine ever made available in the Freelander?

magazine: 'the V6 has a delightful snarl when pressed hard, and I suspect this is going to become as addictive as the characteristic woofle of a Range Rover's V8.' There was a down side, though: 'you need a heavy right foot to extract the best on-road performance, and the transmission's change-up points are set to give only adequate performance.'

It was possible to get more out of the V6 by using the Steptronic automatic's manual over-ride or its 'Sport' mode. In manual mode, electronics took over and changed up a gear before you over-revved the engine – which was a relief as, believe me, I did try hard on those French motorways! But ultimately, to my very great surprise, I found that I much preferred the new BMW-built Td4 diesel to that high-performance V6 petrol engine.

Of course, the Td4 was nowhere near as powerful, with just 112bhp at maximum revs as compared to the 177bhp of the V6, so that delivered a lower top speed. The torque, though, was just unbelievably good. With 192lb ft at a low, 1,750rpm – more than the V6 – and a pretty flat torque curve after that (thanks to the VNT turbocharger technology), it had all the low-down grunt I expected of a Land Rover plus rapid acceleration from high speeds for motorway use. This was the one for me.

An unscheduled motorway dash demonstrated that the Td4 was able to turn in some very respectable cross-country times, too. I was out in a vehicle with one of the Land Rover engineers, who was due to catch the same plane home as me, when we found our route to the airport blocked by a road accident. Traffic was being turned round and sent back in the opposite direction, and so we had to make a big loop around the airport and get at it from the other side. To make it in time (which we did – just), I drove that Td4 Freelander flat-out along the French autoroutes, rarely dropping below an indicated 160km/h (100mph). We were both pretty impressed by the vehicle's performance!

In Britain, few motoring magazines took a serious look at the V6, and most preferred to concentrate on the Td4 models which were obviously going to be the volume sellers. However, the V6 was the only option in North America when the Freelander went on sale there at the end of 2002. So, to get an idea of how the new vehicles were received, I've chosen the *Autocar* test of a Td4-powered Freelander and a fairly typical North American appraisal of the V6 from *Driver Source* in the *Toronto Sunday Sun*.

The *Autocar* verdict on the Td4

Autocar published the results of its characteristically thorough test on a Freelander Td4 in its issue dated November 22, 2000. The vehicle was a five-door Station Wagon with the top equipment level: Steptronic automatic and ES trim. For performance testing, the magazine had visited the Millbrook Proving Ground.

The report began by pointing out that the Td4 was 'probably the most cutting-edge oil-burner you'll find in any 4x4.' Performance, though, was disappointing. 'It's quicker than the old L-series manual we tested, but only just, signing off the sprint to 60mph in a relaxed 14.6 seconds and showing a similar lethargy between 30–70mph (16.1sec). We couldn't get it to crack 100mph on the high-speed bowl, acceleration ceasing at 99mph in top gear.' Also 'mildly disappointing' was the 27.7mpg which the Freelander returned on test, which made it 'thirsty for a diesel'.

Refinement, though, came in for praise. 'It's in a different league when it comes to things like engine noise suppression, throttle response and gearchange quality. The engine itself generates far less din than before, and it's much better damped. So although it may not be that quick, the Td4 is nevertheless a supremely relaxing car to drive, on short or long hauls.'

The revised suspension made an impression, and *Autocar* considered that 'the ride is notably calmer and more fluid than before . . . the steering is also much improved, providing greater feel and less vagueness just off centre.' However, 'the front seat still won't go back far enough for tall drivers' (funny – it never worried me, at 6ft 2in).

However, 'with its extra on-road refinement and already untouchable off-road ability, the Freelander is now the best junior 4x4 you can buy, as well as the best-seller. Its popularity will surely continue to blossom as a result.'

The V6 in Toronto

The *Toronto Sunday Sun* published Peter Brewster's impressions of a V6 Freelander Station Wagon (there were no three-doors in North America then) in its issue dated 28 April 2002. This was a few months after the vehicle had become available through showrooms across the Atlantic.

'Essentially,' wrote Brewster, the Freelander was 'a rugged, compact package that vaguely resembles last year's Honda CR-V in size and appearance, especially from the side.' He gave the vehicle 'A' ratings for performance and brakes, 'B+' for handling and rear seat room, and 'B' ratings for ride and front seat room.

The test vehicle was an SE version with leather upholstery, and the driver's seat 'at first felt hard'. However, 'the cloth seats on the entry-level model, which I tried later at a dealership, felt more comfortable'. There was praise for the headroom front and rear, 'and a six-foot-six friend had more air above his head front and back than in his Range Rover.' Brewster found that there was a 'decent' amount of load-carrying space, and thought that 'trim quality throughout is excellent, though plain.'

The short first and second gears meant that 'launching from rest can be abrupt'. However, once on the move, 'acceleration in automatic is brisk and the manual override lets that revvy little six sing.' The Freelander also showed 'a fairly heroic thirst for regular fuel . . . and a larger gas tank than 60 litres would have been more appropriate to North American distances.' (Land Rover jumped on that criticism as quickly as they could, and a larger tank was introduced on the 2003 models.)

Brewster was not very impressed with the ride quality on the SE model's 17-inch wheels with 225/55 tyres. They were good at speed on the highway, but 'they do little to help the Freelander's naturally taut

This is a North American Freelander on the roads of Iceland, where the media launch ride-and-drive exercise was held.

Another North American Freelander – this time a 2003 SE3 model – demonstrates how little the vehicle rolls under hard cornering.

ride' on the rougher surfaces of city streets. 'Worse, although straight-line grip on snow-covered back-roads was good, the 225/55-series rubber would "skate" on slushy bends. I am sure the 215/65 Wranglers on the 16-inch alloy rims of the S model would not only ride better but provide grip to match the Freelander's off-road credentials.'

In summary, the SE specification was not the best of the bunch. 'The base vehicle is $34,800 and is without question the best value. You can spend another nine grand adding leather, sunroof, stereo upgrades, etc and larger wheels with tires more suited to Bloor St than the bush. But look closely at the S version before being seduced by an SE or an HSE.'

PERFORMANCE FIGURES

Land Rover provides 'typical' performance figures for all of its models and, on the whole, these tend to be on the conservative side. That way, the company is less likely to be sued by an irate customer whose vehicle doesn't live up to an optimistic performance claim!

The motoring magazines – particularly *Autocar* in the UK – conduct independent performance tests and often get more impressive results than Land Rover's claims suggest. However, it is important to remember that these figures are usually obtained from a single vehicle which (it is to be hoped) will have been a good one of its type. Land Rover's own figures are more representative of an average cross-section of vehicles and – as they have all been prepared using the same criteria – probably provide the most reliable data for comparison purposes.

Please note, then, that these are the 'official' Land Rover figures,

and that individual vehicles may perform better. Fuel consumption figures come from tests conducted according to standardised criteria used throughout Europe.

What the Land Rover official figures do not always do is to give a reliable guide to a realistic overall average consumption. For that, take a look at road tests published by reputable journals (such as *Autocar*). Those with heavy or particularly light right feet will do worse or better, respectively!

Land Rover quotes the same figures for three-door and five-door models. In practice, the hardback and Station Wagon models have a better coefficient of drag (Cd) than the Softbacks. However, the difference is small enough to be largely theoretical: the figures are 0.40 for the Softbacks and 0.39 for the fixed-roof models. Diesel models are also heavier than their petrol equivalents, by around 100kg, but this difference is accounted for in the 'official' figures.

	1.8 petrol (1998–2001)	2.0 diesel (1998–2001)
Standing start acceleration (0–60mph)	1.1sec	14.6sec
Max speed	102mph (165km/h)	96mph (155km/h)
Fuel economy		
Urban cycle	21.7mpg (13.0 l/100km)	29.6mpg (9.6 l/100km)
Extra urban	32.8mpg (8.6 l/100km)	42.4mpg (6.7 l/100km)
Combined	27.6mpg (10.2 l/100km)	36.6mpg (7.7 l/100km)

	1.8 petrol (2001 on)	V6
Standing start acceleration (0–60mph)	11. 8 sec	10.1 sec
Max speed	106mph (170km/h)	113mph (182km/h)
Fuel economy		
Urban cycle	20.8mpg (13.6 l/100km)	16.5mpg (17.1 l/100km)
Extra urban	33.3mpg (8.5 l/100km)	29.1mpg (9.7 l/100km)
Combined	27.3mpg (10.4 l/100km)	22.7mpg (12.4 l/100km)

	Td4 (manual)	Td4 (automatic)
Standing start acceleration (0–60mph)	13.2 sec	14.3 sec
Max speed	102mph (164km/h)	100mph (161km/h)
Fuel economy		
Urban cycle	31.0mpg (9.11 l/100km)	25.2mpg (11.2 l/100km)
Extra urban	42.2mpg (6.7 l/100km)	39.5mpg (7.1 l/100km)
Combined	37.2mpg (7.6 l/100km)	32.7mpg (8.6 l/100km)

Chapter **Nine**

Freelander off-road

The Freelander's off-road ability has been a subject of controversy among die-hard Land Rover enthusiasts and others who enjoy off-road driving, ever since the model was announced in 1997. It is unfortunate that most of those who set themselves up as bar-room experts on the matter have never actually driven a Freelander at all, let alone off-road, and that their opinions are based on a mixture of hearsay, misunderstanding and theory.

So saying, no-one should run away with the idea that a Freelander is every bit the equal of Land Rover's traditional off-roaders – the Defender (and its utility forebears), the Discovery, and the Range Rover. It isn't. But the majority of people who are used to off-road driving with these vehicles and others of their type come away very impressed from the experience of driving a Freelander off-road. Most will say that the Freelander performs much better than its paper specification suggests, while those whose experience is wide enough for their comments to carry some weight will claim that it out-performs all of its direct rivals.

Of course, the competition is hotting up. The Freelander's huge success has persuaded other manufacturers to offer competitive models, and as these get better and better, so the Freelander will no longer be the best in its class. By then, though, if all goes according to plan, Land Rover should have the second-generation Freelander ready to go and the competition will start all over again.

A look back at the origins of the Freelander in Chapter One shows how much hesitation there was in the beginning about giving the new entry-level Land Rover proper off-road ability. There were those who thought it would be better off wearing Rover badges and not pretending to be an off-roader at all. But as soon as the decision had been taken that the new

model should be called a Land Rover, there could be no question about it: it would have to live up to public expectations of the Land Rover name. If it failed to do so, it would undermine the public image of existing and planned Land Rover products.

There were arguments – or 'creative tensions' as the public relations people would prefer it – and in the end the result was a Great British Compromise. The Freelander would have real off-road ability but in giving it that ability the designers must not compromise its road performance, its chic appeal, or its manufacturing cost. As the entry-level model in the Land Rover range, it could afford not to be quite as good as the senior models. And that is why the Freelander is not as capable as other Land Rovers off-road, and was never intended to be.

What makes a good off-road vehicle?

To understand the Freelander's off-road abilities and shortcomings, it's important to put it into context. With the basic requirements of a good off-road vehicle clearly in mind, it's easier to see how the entry-level Land Rover shapes up.

The number one requirement for any four-wheeled vehicle intended for use away from metalled roads is that it should have *drive to all of its wheels*. This doubles its chance of obtaining and retaining grip on loose surfaces as compared to a four-wheeled vehicle with only two driven wheels. In some ways, the comparison is the same as that between a man and a donkey. Donkeys can climb steep mountain tracks because their four legs give them a better chance of getting a grip on the terrain, but a man with just two legs often finds he has to use his hands to help him.

The next requirement is that the vehicle must have *plenty of engine torque* (turning power), so that there is

The Freelander makes an ideal vehicle for greenlaning activities. Although the terrain visible through the windscreen here is not rough, the mud would quickly stop an ordinary car.

plenty of effort available at the wheels when it is needed. Driving fast in difficult terrain is usually impossible and at best foolhardy, so this high torque needs to be available at low engine speeds for when the vehicle is moving slowly.

This need to drive slowly, often while checking the ground ahead for obstacles, demands a degree of *control* which is not usually available in conventional road vehicles. Off-road vehicles have traditionally provided this control through a set of low-ratio gears. These allow a vehicle to be driven very slowly down a steep slope while still under full control, and they also

One of the Freelander's off-road limitations is its restricted ground clearance. The front guard plate is likely to ground out very frequently.

multiply the torque available at the wheels to give additional effort for negotiating uphill slopes.

Away from metalled roads, the surface the vehicle is driving on is likely to be rough. There may be deep ditches and ruts, and also small boulders, tree branches and other obstructions on the track; there may also be areas where the ground rises steeply. To counter these difficulties, a good off-roader needs two things: *high ground clearance and long suspension travel.*

The ground clearance of a vehicle is usually defined as the distance between the ground and the lowest part of the vehicle's underside (not including the wheel hubs). On a low-slung sports car, this lowest part is often the exhaust silencer – and, sadly, that is also the case with some vehicles which pretend to be off-roaders. On a good off-roader, the lowest part is likely to be an axle differential, everything else being tucked up out of harm's way. This is why off-roaders usually stand higher off the ground than conventional cars.

Suspension travel is the distance that a vehicle's wheel can travel between full 'bump' (when the wheel is pushed up into the wheelarch as far as it will go) and full 'rebound' (when it is hanging down as far as the suspension will allow it to). The advantage of long-travel suspension on an off-road vehicle is that it provides an increased chance that a wheel or wheels on full rebound will retain contact with the ground in extreme terrain and so provide the traction required to keep the vehicle moving.

Related to all this is the question of *suspension type*. Land Rovers and many other off-road vehicles have traditionally used beam axles – with the wheels at either end of solid axles – because these offer the best chances of retaining contact with the ground in rough terrain. For example, imagine a six-inch (ie, not very large) tree trunk lying halfway across a track. If the left-hand front wheel hits it and is pushed up into the wheelarch, there is a corresponding downward movement of the right-hand front wheel which also lifts the centre of the vehicle up. This allows the vehicle the best chance of driving over that tree-trunk.

By contrast, independent suspension does not give this advantage. Visualise that same left-hand front wheel hitting the tree-trunk and being pushed up into the wheelarch. There is no corresponding movement of the right-hand front wheel, so the front of the vehicle remains level, contacts the tree-trunk and prevents the vehicle from being driven over it.

Modern electronic control systems allow the best of both worlds. The independent suspension fitted to the

current Range Rover, for example, gives all the desirable on-road handling characteristics associated with independent systems and behaves like beam axles off-road to give the best possible chance of clearing obstacles.

It is also important for an off-road vehicle to wear *suitable tyres*. The tyres are the only point of contact between a vehicle and the ground, and they must provide grip over a wide range of different surfaces. 'Road' tyres are designed to give good adhesion between tyre and metalled road surface. Their tread patterns are designed to siphon standing rainwater away from the contact area as quickly as possible to

This is the kind of terrain which can stop a Freelander without ETC, although it looks relatively easy. The problem is that limited suspension travel will prevent the wheel from dropping into the ditch and finding traction. If the same happens on the diagonally opposite rear wheel, as well it might, the differentials will divert all the driving force to the two spinning wheels and the vehicle will stop.

ensure that the tyre makes contact with the road surface and does not 'aquaplane' or run on a film of water.

However, mud and other loose debris can quickly clog the treads of a tyre off-road, and so tyres designed for off-road use typically have a more open tread pattern which reduces this clogging. The raised parts of the tread may also be more aggressively designed to give better grip on soft surfaces: think of a tractor tyre to get the picture here. Tyres designed purely for off-road use tend to be noisy on metalled roads, to wear rapidly and to give poor adhesion in cornering.

As a result, most of today's dual-purpose off-roaders wear compromise tyres which give a good account of themselves both on the road and off it, but do not give the ultimate performance in either set of circumstances. Off-road driving enthusiasts often keep a second set of tyres on a spare set of wheels and fit these before taking their everyday driver into the rough.

How does the Freelander shape up?

The Freelander does have *drive to all its four wheels*. This drive is permanently engaged (on some off-roaders, the drive to the front wheels can be disengaged for ordinary road use). The vehicle has a torque-biasing system – described in Chapter Two – which allows driving effort to be distributed to the wheels which

Wheelspin must start before the ETC will cut in, as the system is reactive rather than pro-active. In certain circumstances, this can allow a vehicle to dig itself into soft ground and make further movement difficult.

need it most. Permanent four-wheel drive is a standard feature of all current Land Rover products.

When all four wheels are connected to the power source (engine), they do not all turn at exactly the same speed. Differences between one side and another (such as occur, for example, when the wheels on the outside of a bend have to travel further than those on the inside) are absorbed by the conventional axle differentials. However, speed differences can also occur between front and rear pairs of wheels, and if there is no mechanism to permit this, the results will be either excessive tyre wear (caused by scrub) or damage to the drivetrain. To prevent this, a centre differential may be fitted between the front and rear pairs of wheels.

However, on loose surfaces off-road, maximum traction is often obtained by locking this centre differential. The effect of this is to distribute the driving effort more evenly across all four wheels, so increasing the chances that traction will be maintained.

Freelanders have no centre differential, and front-to-rear speed differences are absorbed by the viscous coupling in the Intermediate Reduction Drive (IRD). However, the effect of locking the centre differential is replicated to a large degree by the Electronic Traction Control (ETC) system – which was not fitted to some

FREELANDER AND THE G4 CHALLENGE

The Land Rover G4 Challenge was announced in late July 2002. Based to some extent on the old Camel Trophy and the TReK annual dealer-team competition, it was essentially a marketing ploy to bring the Land Rover brand to the attention of potential buyers whose hobbies included such things as orienteering, trail running, kayaking and mountain biking. Competitors had to participate in all these activities and more – including a limited amount of off-road driving in Land Rovers – with the aim of proving that they had the best combination of physical skill, 4x4 driving abilities, up-for-it attitude and strategic thinking capability.

The 2003 G4 Challenge was held in four locations across three different continents. The G in the title stood for Global, the 4 for the four locations. These were the East and West Coasts of the USA, South Africa, and Australia. Competitors from 16 nations took part, a single representative of each nation having been chosen to go through to the finals from selection trials held in each participating country at the end of 2002.

All four Land Rover ranges – Freelander, Defender, Discovery and Range Rover – were represented on the Challenge. Of the 154 vehicles in total (including four prototypes and six workshop-equipped Discoverys), 29 were Freelanders. All were V6 models, finished in Tangiers Orange and equipped with low-line roof racks, Warn lights mounted on these racks, a receiver hitch front and rear for a demountable winch, and underbody protection. They were also fitted with the latest Goodyear MT/R all-terrain tyres.

The Land Rover G4 Challenge was a 2003 promotional event which featured all four of Solihull's model ranges. The Freelander certainly looked the part . . .

Of those 29 Freelanders, one was a prototype – built early in 2002 – and the other 28 were used on the overseas legs of the event. These were built in mid-2002 and were equipped by Land Rover's Vehicle Operations division at Gaydon. Of those 28, 20 were shipped to the USA, four to South Africa and four to Australia. However, none of the Freelanders was destined to be used by the competitors; all of them had been built as 'support' vehicles to carry event management teams and members of the media who would be reporting on the event.

. . . and the G4 vehicles were even fitted with receiver hitches for a demountable winch, although Land Rover declined to make these available through the showrooms.

early low-spec models. As soon as a wheel loses traction and starts to spin, it is automatically braked through the ABS system. This transfers the driving effort to the opposite side wheel through the action of the 'axle' differential, and if this wheel still has traction the vehicle will remain mobile.

Effective as the ETC system is, it is not quite as good as a traditional locking centre differential. Though it certainly operates almost instantaneously, it is a reactive system – that is, it will not operate until wheelspin has already begun and traction has been lost. In some circumstances that can be too late. A centre differential, on the other hand, is a proactive system: it allows the driver to anticipate a loss of traction and to take counter-action to avoid it.

All models of Freelander offer quite good low-down *engine torque*. Although every engine in the range – the 1.8 and 2.5-litre petrol types, and the L-series and Td4 diesels – was originally designed as a car engine, each one has been re-tuned for its Freelander application to maximise bottom-end torque. Some, though, are better than others.

Modern car engines typically deliver their maximum torque at speeds of 3,000–4,000rpm or higher to give good acceleration at high motorway speeds. The Freelander engines give their maximum torque at 1,750rpm (Td4 diesel), 2,000rpm (L-series diesel), 2,750rpm (1.8 petrol), and 4,000rpm (V6). Although the V6 engine also delivers strong torque lower down the rev range, it is easy to see from this comparison which are the best engines for off-road use! However, the same figures cannot be used to give an accurate comparison of which engines are best for on-road use. In particular, the Td4 develops very nearly the same torque at low revs as it does at high ones and is in many respects the best of the Freelander engines for on-road use as well as off-road.

The Freelander does not use the traditional systems for off-road *control*. It does not have a set of low-ratio gears but instead, relies on a fairly low first gear in the main gearbox and on its patented Hill Descent Control (HDC) system. It should therefore be quite obvious that early low-spec Freelanders without this system are not best suited for off-road use.

Relying on a low first gear (roughly equivalent to Low Fourth in a traditional system with off-road crawler gears) means that in some off-road conditions the Freelander can feel over-geared. When driving at very low speeds, drivers find that the only way to increase engine revs to get more torque is to slip the clutch. As a

result, many Freelander owners who use their vehicles a lot off-road find that they are renewing clutch linings more frequently than they otherwise might.

HDC is a remarkable system, but drivers brought up to use a traditional low-ratio gearset often take some time to acclimatise to it. In a nutshell, they find it hard to trust the system until it has proved itself, and they are unwilling to let it prove itself because they don't trust it! However, once the necessary trust has been established, HDC will automatically limit a Freelander's downhill speed in first or reverse gear, thus providing a high degree of the controllability which is necessary in an off-road vehicle.

There is no doubt that the Freelander does have a greater *ground clearance* than most conventional cars, with 186mm (7.32in) under its front end. Equally, there is no doubt that it does not have as much ground clearance as its fellows from the Land Rover stable; a Discovery, for example, has a minimum 208mm (8.2in) of clearance. This, then, is one of the factors which makes it less capable off-road than they are.

It is also true that the Freelander may sustain minor damage off-road more readily than other Land Rover products. At the front, its steering and sump are protected by a standard guard plate, but the transverse exhaust silencer at the rear is particularly vulnerable to grounding if the vehicle has to climb steeply. Anyone planning to use a Freelander for much off-road work would therefore be well-advised to fit an aftermarket exhaust guard (usually known as a 'bash plate').

The Freelander's *suspension travel* is longer than that of most conventional cars, thus giving it the best chance of retaining traction if one wheel drops into a ditch or gully. However, it is not as long as the travel provided by the Discovery's suspension, and this limits the Freelander's off-road ability to a degree. The entry-level Land Rover also does not have the ideal *suspension type* for off-road work. It uses an all-round independent suspension to give it the best possible handling characteristics on the road – completely in line with its designers' intentions. This system does not benefit from the electronic control applied to the current Range Rover, which is too expensive for a vehicle in the Freelander's price bracket. Many of its off-road limitations stem from this.

Lastly, as far as *tyres* are concerned, the Freelander comes as standard with tyres which are no better and no worse than those fitted to other Land Rover products as standard equipment. They are a compromise type, giving good roadholding and low road noise while offering a reasonable standard of grip for off-road use. However, they will clog with mud quite easily, and this of course reduces their ability to grip. There are relatively few tyres with an off-road bias on the market that are suitable for use on Freelanders, although that situation is likely to change over the next few years.

So, how much does the design of the Freelander help or limit its off-road abilities? Its four-wheel drive system and long-travel suspension are plus points, while its HDC is an ingenious solution to the problem of controlling speed on downhill slopes. Quite good low-down torque from all its engines – although some are better than others – is another point in its favour.

On the down side, though, it lacks a low range of gears for certain types of off-road work and its ground clearance is average, rather than good. The lack of a lockable centre differential can further limit its ability to keep going in some circumstances. Its standard tyres are a compromise and, while that can be said of all current Land Rover products, the fact is that Freelander owners do not yet have a good choice of alternative off-road rubber.

Even so, as noted earlier, the Freelander tends to surprise seasoned off-roaders who drive it over rough

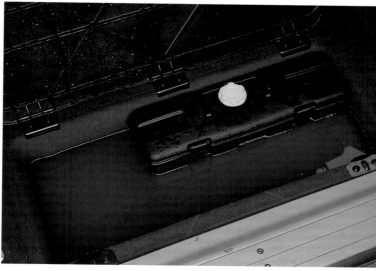

Sadly, build quality doesn't always allow the Freelander to live up to its promise. This was what happened to the underfloor rear stowage compartment of a 2001 Freelander which was taken through water on an off-road course.

A Freelander's off-road ability has surprised doubters on many occasions.

terrain for the first time. So what effect do those theoretical limitations caused by its design have on the vehicle in practice?

What you can and can't do with a Freelander off-road

My friend and colleague Martin Hodder put it like this in the November 2000 issue of *LAND ROVER enthusiast* magazine:

'Provided it is fitted with ETC (which works in conjunction with the ABS) a Freelander is surprisingly competent over very slippery surfaces which will stop even a Defender with conventional transmission. Therefore, a Freelander can be outstanding on slippery grass-covered slopes, muddy hills, snow and ice – which are the typical-use conditions the design team had in mind.

'The Hill Descent Control (HDC) enables it to cope with the same conditions downhill, again outperforming some other Land Rovers because of the finesse afforded through this intelligent application of advanced technology.

'However, the HDC can be inadequate on extreme off-road downhill terrain, when the speed of descent, which is controlled to 5.6mph, might be too fast. In comparison, a Tdi-powered vehicle [the Tdi is a diesel engine used in other Land Rovers] relying on engine braking in the same situation would be travelling at no more than 4mph.

'What all this means is that a Freelander, especially when equipped with ABS and ETC, is capable of tackling many greenlanes, but only where there are no deep ruts which cannot be straddled, and no deep ditches or washouts running across the direction of its travel.

'As a caravan or trailer tug it's an excellent machine . . . because of its ability to keep moving over rain-soaked grass or moderately-deep mud. And for everyday transport in hilly districts prone to snow and frost, it is just about unbeatable.

'Just don't expect it to keep going when things get really bad!'

Here's Martin again, summarising the Freelander's off-road behaviour in the September 2001 issue of our magazine:

Left: A Freelander makes a competent recreational off-roader, but does not have all the abilities of its Land Rover stable-mates.

'. . . the Freelander is handicapped at those times when ground clearance and very slow speed are major factors. Situations likely to cause problems include: deep ruts; deep mud over a potholed or rock-strewn surface; very rough ground which causes cross-axled situations; ditches; ridges; large rocks and boulders.

'However, in many other situations – those that the average owner is more likely to encounter – the Freelander excels and is sometimes able to keep going where many other four-wheel drive vehicles might well stop.

'. . . of particular value is ETC, which gives the vehicle exceptional performance in those situations which, although not extreme, are most likely to cause problems to the Freelander driver – wet, grassy slopes; muddy hillsides; snow and ice. A Freelander thus equipped can often sail unhindered up a greasy, mud-covered climb that would have a Defender really struggling.'

What could have been added here is that the Freelander's automatic traction control systems are more than a match for the abilities of the average or novice off-road driver in a theoretically better-equipped vehicle. However, a competent off-road driver in a Defender should always have an advantage over a similarly skilled driver in a Freelander.

There's an important difference between driving a Freelander off-road and driving other Land Rover products off-road, too, and veteran trials driver Dave Barker (assistant editor of *LAND ROVER enthusiast*) quickly identified it. In the magazine's April 2002 issue, he wrote:

'If you have ever been taken off-roading in a Freelander by Land Rover's own Demonstration Team (and I recommend this), the first thing you notice is the speed they drive at. It's quite different from the slow and steady speed used in other vehicles. Once the Freelander is stuck, you need to keep the engine revving and the wheels spinning. This gives the traction control a chance to work at its best and with any luck you'll regain traction to pull the vehicle out of trouble.

'The one exception is when you have a couple of wheels off the ground, which is easily done due to the lack of axle articulation. However, with practice you develop a different driving style when off-roading a Freelander. Reading the ground becomes

Using Freelanders on the 1998 Camel Trophy boosted the vehicle's credibility as an off-roader, although such driving was not as challenging that year as it had been on earlier events. Here, a pre-production Freelander is seen on the recce for the event.

FREELANDER AND THE CAMEL TROPHY

Between 1982 and 1998, Land Rover was co-sponsor of an annual off-road adventure called the Camel Trophy. This took its name from the brand of adventure clothing produced by an offshoot of the RJ Reynolds tobacco company (makers of Camel cigarettes), who were the co-sponsors.

For Land Rover, the Camel Trophy was first and foremost a public relations exercise. It pitted teams of two from several nations (typically, around 16 nations would be represented) against one another, and was based on a long-distance driving expedition for which Land Rover provided the specially equipped vehicles. These were always kitted out with a variety of off-road equipment and were invariably painted in Camel Trophy Yellow (which was in fact the old British Leyland colour called Sandglow).

The expedition typically took in swathes of terrain which showcased the Land Rovers' off-road abilities, and included special sections where the competitors had to demonstrate other outdoor skills. Photographs from the event were used to reinforce the Land Rover image of all-terrain invincibility.

However, things changed on the 1997 event. Mountain biking and kayaking sections took a much greater prominence alongside the driving elements of the Camel Trophy, and many enthusiasts believed it had gone 'soft'. In fact, the focus was changing because on the 1998 event, Land Rover planned to use Freelanders. It was clear that these were not as rugged as the Discoverys which had been the backbone of the event for so long, and so less prominence had to be given to the heavy-duty off-road driving elements of the

Camel Trophy. The individuals who represented their nations had to work no less hard than before, and were no less deserving of the awards they won — but the focus on Land Rovers which had made the Camel Trophy such a draw for enthusiasts worldwide was gone.

The 1998 event, known as Camel Trophy — Tierra del Fuego, was actually held in Chile and Argentina, and in fact, the Freelanders played a very limited role in it. Of the 10 Freelanders shipped out to Chile for the event, only three were actually used by the competing teams, the others being reserved for 'event management' — which really meant the PR officers and journalists who were invited along for the ride. Off-road driving played an even smaller part in the event than it had in 1997, and more prominence was given to testing the competitors' abilities at canoeing, ski-ing and mountain climbing.

After this event, Land Rover withdrew its sponsorship of the Camel Trophy — but its absence was keenly felt by the company's marketing people, who came up with a new event for 2002 which they hoped would replace it as an international draw. This was the Land Rover G4 Challenge (see page 115).

The Camel Trophy Freelanders were modified by the Freelander engineering team in conjunction with Safety Devices, and the project was managed by Land Rover Special Vehicles. Their special features included an internal roll cage, one-inch spacers in the suspension to cope with the extra load, an aluminium sump guard, a demountable winch (normally stowed in the back, where wire cages were used to restrain the load), a snorkel, a unique roof rack (which used the standard fixings), a light pod, and various emergency shut-off switches. The Camel Trophy Freelanders had standard tyres on 16-inch wheels, and most were probably pre-production vehicles, as they were taken off the lines in September 1997.

Right: One of the Freelanders used on the 1998 Camel Trophy is seen here in testing conditions. Even without snow chains, an ETC-equipped Freelander performs superbly in snow; with chains, it is virtually unstoppable.

much more important, and you find yourself looking harder for the best route as you understand the vehicle's strengths and limitations.'

Of course, not all off-road driving is about mud-plugging; that is a peculiarly British preoccupation and probably results largely from our weather. In other countries, such as North America, Australia and South Africa, off-road driving is a rather different sort of pastime.

In North America, a favourite off-road recreation is rock-crawling – driving a 4x4 vehicle across impossible-looking piles of rocks and boulders. This demands both high ground clearance and first-rate low-speed control – neither of them among the Freelander's good points. Nevertheless, the Freelander is ideal for the other American favourite of trail driving, which tends to focus on unsurfaced tracks (such as old logging trails on mountain sides) where good traction and manoeuvrability are needed, but where high ground clearance and low gear ratios are less important.

In Australia and South Africa, off-road driving is different again. In these vast countries, 4x4 vehicles are often used as transport for exploring the wilderness – where a GPS to find your location and a satellite phone to call for help are among the most important items of equipment to take with you. The Freelander has not proved popular in Australia – where being launched with the feeble 1.8-litre petrol engine instead of waiting for the powerful V6 did it no favours – but it has gone down well in South Africa. So well, in fact, that Freelanders are now being built in South Africa from kits of parts shipped out from Solihull (see Chapter Six). These vehicles are being sold in southern Africa and are also being used to meet demand in Australia.

So perhaps the last words on off-road driving in a Freelander should go to Christopher Race, *LAND ROVER enthusiast* magazine's senior representative in southern Africa. In the June 2002 issue, he reported on a trip with a five-door Td4 manual-gearbox model of nearly 1,000 miles: 'over highway, lowveld bush roads and seriously forgotten mountain tracks – pioneer trails where prospectors once roamed for gold.' He wrote:

'The Freelander is just too much for the mind; like a rail up the trail. It has to be the steadiest little number we've had on the dirt and you have to really abuse it before it even begins to feel unseated. Those long corners were a joy; hit them hard and the tail swings out slightly. Then, it just gets back into line again – every time.

'The independent suspension handles really deep ruts and runnels with ease and the power steering is beautifully weighted and balanced. There's very little body shake and superb visibility. Though the rear silencer looks vulnerable, we never bottomed it. One wonders, however, how long it will take the pounding it must get from stones and the rest.'

However, on the mountain trails near Tzaneen, Christopher encountered some problems.

'Several in fact. It started with the way the Freelander looks and feels. It's the sort of car that makes you want to go there – wherever "there" is. In short, it does what a Land Rover should do – it rattles the adventure genes.

'Problem is, once embarked down adventure lane, it starts to run out of green oval in two departments – the cogs and the clutch. Where other Land Rovers have an extra set of gear ratios, this one ain't. And where other Land Rovers have an entirely workaholic clutch, this one has something modelled on Formula One lines.

'Enter problem number three – the electrickery. It works. It does exactly what it says on the packaging. Factor in the Hill Descent Control, the Electronic Traction Control, et al, and down you go, all in order. It's the getting back that can be embarrassing.

'Land Rover's Freelander spec book assures the user that the little beauty will hill start – forward or backwards – on a 33° slope. This it does on tar and probably on a firm, dry surface. Inviting little tracks seldom have either. What they do have where we come from is terrain that is loose and often slippery. It requires slow traversing and gear ratios that harness engine torque in the right way.

'Enter problem number four – the Td4 engine just hates doing anything once the revs drop below 2000. Remedy . . . boot it over 2000 and use the clutch. Response pretty damn quick – the clutch smells like hell.

'We bottled out 30km down one perfect trail, after assessing the second decisive downward slope. It was way up on top of the Drakensberg . . . the road becomes a track which calls you on. But not in a Freelander.'

Where to try your Freelander off-road

First of all, don't let anyone tell you that you're not a proper Land Rover enthusiast because you've never driven your Freelander off-road. You don't have to do it, any more than you have to drive a high-performance sports car at its maximum speed.

On the other hand, trying your Freelander off-road is an experience I'd recommend. If you decide it's not for you, then all well and good. If you decide you enjoy it, then you've discovered another dimension to ownership of your Freelander.

Off-road driving takes many forms, and some of them are competitive. At one end of the spectrum there are long-distance international rally-raids – the best-known being the annual Paris–Dakar event – and at the other end there are mildly challenging club trials which test a driver's skill in manoeuvring his or her vehicle around canes and through difficult terrain. If these are what interest you, then the bad news is that your Freelander isn't the best vehicle for the job.

However, recreational off-road driving is not competitive, and it can be both rewarding and relaxing. The reward comes from successfully negotiating a tricky patch of ground; the relaxation can come from a gentle drive through unspoiled countryside on a summer afternoon – but before you decide that's for you, please do read the notes which follow on where you can legally drive off-road.

As a first step, I'd recommend getting some professional off-road driving tuition. There are schools for this all over the UK, and you can easily track them down through the magazines aimed at off-road driving enthusiasts. (There are similar schools in many overseas countries too, although the situation varies from place to place.) Land Rover itself runs Land Rover Experience Centres, and if you're buying a brand-new Freelander from a Land Rover dealership, you will

Freelanders on a club greenlane outing in Britain – or should that be a 'white lane' outing in this case?

automatically be offered the chance to enrol for a day's off-road driving tuition at one of these.

One way or another, you'd be silly to head off into the countryside hoping for off-road excitement until you've been shown how to drive your Freelander properly. You might get stuck, which would be embarrassing for you. You might also do some quite unnecessary damage to the ground you drive on, which would discourage the landowner from letting other 4x4 drivers use his land in the future. And driving on private land without permission would, of course, open you to the possibility of prosecution for trespass.

One of the things which a day's professional tuition

Never wade a Freelander in water any deeper than the top of the wheel rim (unless it has been specially prepared for the job). Water is likely to get into the engine air intake and down into the combustion chambers, where it will cause expensive damage.

will teach you is proper respect for the environment. We've all heard tales of hooligans in off-road vehicles smashing down gates or fences and carving deep ruts in a track which make it impassable for horses and walkers. Land Rover itself is implacably opposed to such behaviour, and the company was a founder member of the Tread Lightly organisation in North America, which encourages 4x4 drivers to minimise the impact they have on the environment and to respect others' rights to enjoy it. In the UK, this approach is embodied in what the company calls its Fragile Earth policy. Any Land Rover dealership should be able to supply you with a leaflet which contains the essentials of this.

When you think you know what you're doing, you might decide to head off into the countryside with a small number of other 4x4 owners. Joining a club is the best way to meet such people, and most of them are very friendly indeed. It's only fair to warn you, though,

that there are die-hards in some of the Land Rover clubs who simply can't accept that a Freelander *is* a Land Rover – or indeed an off-road vehicle at all. They are sad cases, because they spoil a lot of people's fun and ultimately bring their own enthusiast movement into disrepute, but there's no denying that they exist and can make you feel most unwelcome.

It's worth bearing in mind that the laws about driving in the countryside differ from country to country, and that before you set off with your Freelander you should make sure you know what is permitted and what isn't. In the UK, especially, the laws about driving on unsurfaced tracks (often known generically as 'greenlanes', although the law categorises them into several different types) are an absolute minefield. The most sensible thing to do if you want to go greenlaning in the UK is to contact your local 4x4 club for advice, or perhaps to speak to LARA (Land and Recreational Association) or GLASS (Green Lane Association). Their current contact addresses appear regularly in magazines devoted to 4x4 matters.

These are the critical dimensions to be aware of when off-roading in a Freelander, as shown in a Land Rover sales brochure. You don't have to learn them parrot-fashion, but a rough knowledge will stop you demanding too much of the vehicle.

Capabilities

Approach/departure angles

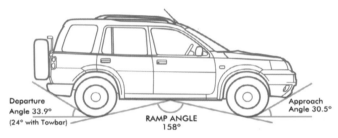

Departure Angle 33.9° (24° with Towbar)

RAMP ANGLE 158°

Approach Angle 30.5°

Wading depth

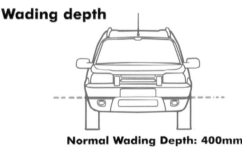

Normal Wading Depth: 400mm

Obstacle clearance

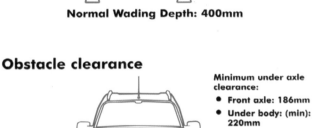

Minimum under axle clearance:
- **Front axle: 186mm**
- **Under body: (min): 220mm**
- **Rear axle: 214mm**
- **Front Suspension Articulation: 180mm**
- **Rear Suspension Articulation: 240mm**

Hill start

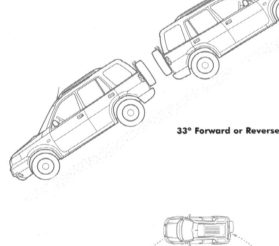

33° Forward or Reverse

Minimum kerb-kerb turning: 11.6m 3.2 turns of wheel

Chapter Ten

Choosing and buying

Your own Freelander

If everything that has been said about the Freelander so far makes you absolutely sure that you want one, then now is the time to take a break. No matter how hard you try when you come to buying, heart will probably rule over head (and if it doesn't, you're probably a sad case) – but if you allow time for your enthusiasm to cool down just a little, you will probably find that some of the things your head is telling you will make sense.

First of all, you need to establish how much you can realistically afford to spend on your Freelander. If you can stretch to a brand-new one – probably aided by a bank loan, overdraft, or some sort of hire-purchase or leasing deal – then you're in a very fortunate position. Most people reading this probably won't be as lucky as you are, and they'll have to watch their pennies a little more carefully. Even so, don't run away with the idea

Practical stowage is provided by nets like this, a feature which the Freelander borrowed from its Discovery stable-mate.

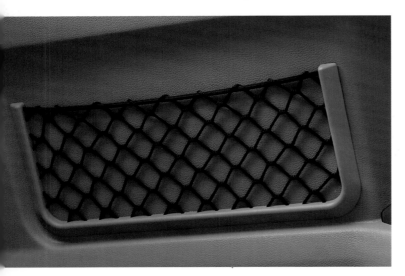

that money buys happiness. It's still worth your while skimming through this chapter to make sure that you do get the Freelander which suits your needs best.

Why do you want a Freelander?

If you're going to end up with the right vehicle, it's best to start with a clear understanding of what you're really aiming at. It isn't always easy to define exactly why you want a particular model – heart is ruling head again – but you'll help yourself no end if you can pin down exactly what it is you're after. That way, you won't end up with a Freelander which disappoints because it doesn't have some of the features that you really wanted.

Some people buy Freelanders because they are stylish. If that's you, try to think through exactly what you mean by 'stylish'. Do you mean that the vehicle itself has a style which appeals to you, or do you mean that the vehicle makes an ideal platform for the sort of style accoutrements (see Chapter Eleven) which you would like? There's a big difference.

Some people buy Freelanders because they're practical. Again, if that's you, define exactly what you mean by 'practical'. Are you talking about practicality in load-carrying, in people-carrying, or in all-weather and all-terrain ability? Some of those factors will make a difference to which model of Freelander you really want to buy.

Then there's the idea that Freelanders are fun. If that's what appeals to you, make sure you know exactly what sort of 'fun' you're after. If your idea of 'fun' means summer weekends with the roof off and the windows down, then you don't want a five-door Station Wagon. If you don't like the idea of having a soft top in the winter rain and snow, perhaps you should think about a Hardback – or perhaps you should

aim for a three-door which has both Softback and Hardback equipment.

You might be one of those people who genuinely intend to use your Freelander off-road – sometimes. Be realistic about what you expect to do with it, and re-read Chapter Eight. A Freelander is a very competent off-road vehicle but it isn't the ultimate mud-plugger. Make sure you're not expecting more of the vehicle than it was ever designed to give.

OK – still sure you want a Freelander? Then it's time to decide which model to go for.

Three-door or five-door? The open-backed three-door model is of course ideally suited to sunny climates . . .

. . . but the five-door model can offer nearly as much fun, as this picture from a publicity shoot associated with the model's Australian launch makes clear.

Three-door or five-door?

The fundamental choice in buying a Freelander is between the three-door and five-door models. There is, of course, also the Commercial – but you'll know whether you want one of those or not.

This decision is a very important one. Although both models share the same mechanical elements and have many other features in common, they actually have almost totally different characters.

The three-door model was always aimed at younger buyers, typically without children, and it was designed to meet what Land Rover saw as their needs. If you think of it as a 2+2 rather than a four- or five-seater, you'll get a clearer idea of what it's all about. There

certainly is enough room in the back for two or three passengers, depending on the seating configuration, but those rear seats are best regarded as 'occasional'. The angled window pillar means that those sitting in the back don't get a good view out, and this can become tiresome on long journeys.

Then there's the question of the roof arrangements on a three-door. The Softback operates very effectively, and is generally water-tight, but you're asking for trouble if you leave your Softback Freelander parked in

the street overnight in many areas. It's all too easy for someone to slash the fabric or the plastic 'windows', either to get at what you've left inside the vehicle or purely for a laugh. The Softback is not cheap to replace.

The Hardback makes for a more permanent-feeling arrangement and it isn't as vulnerable to damage as the Softback. Equally, it takes a lot longer to remove a Hardback to turn your three-door Freelander into an open-backed car – and then, where are you going to leave the Hardback when it isn't in use?

Turning now to the five-door, it's important to recognise that this model was deliberately designed for family users. The extra doors give better access to the rear seats (although there isn't actually any more room

The three-door Freelander is a great fun vehicle, but that thick pillar behind the doors and the angled pillar further back do restrict the view out for rear-seat passengers.

in the back), and the fixed roof gives that feeling of security which family buyers like. The interior has a few extra pockets and cubbies where you can hide family clutter, and the standard upholstery is altogether more sober than that of the three-door type.

The five-door wasn't designed as a 'fun' vehicle in the same way as the three-door. Although it may offer more fun than the small conventional estate cars to which it provides an alternative, it doesn't have the open-air dimension which is so much a part of the three-door Freelander. If what you really want is a three-door Freelander, you'll find a five-door dull and ordinary.

Which engine?

The question of which engine to have is likely to be influenced to a large extent by your financial position. Diesels will offer cheaper running costs, but everybody wants them and so the initial purchase price is likely to be higher than that of a comparable petrol-powered model – the flagship V6 model excluded, of course. Then there's the issue of which diesel to have: the Td4 is very much preferable to the earlier L-series, but it's only been available since Autumn 2000 and so Td4-powered Freelanders are newer and therefore automatically more expensive than the older models.

It is worth looking at the pros and cons of each engine in turn, so that you can make an informed decision. Even though you may have to rule out some engines, at least you'll know what to expect from the one or ones you've ruled in.

Let's start with the *1.8-litre petrol engine*. It comes in two guises, the pre-2001 type and the later type. Both variants are essentially the same engine, the main differences being that the later ones have been modified to meet stricter exhaust emissions control requirements.

The later engines are also slightly less powerful and deliver less torque. Early 1.8-litre engines have 118bhp at 5,550rpm and 121lb ft of torque at 2,750rpm; the 2001 and later types have 115bhp at 5,500rpm and 118lb ft at the same 2,750rpm. To be quite honest, the differences are not noticeable in everyday driving, so you can disregard them.

The 1.8-litre engine will feel reassuringly familiar to anyone who's been used to driving a typical modern small car with an engine of between about 1.3 and 1.6 litres' capacity. It needs the extra couple of hundred cubic centimetres of swept volume to compensate for the extra weight and aerodynamic drag of the Freelander, so don't expect more sparkling performance.

However, what you can expect is a free-revving power unit which is likely to sound a bit thrashy at high speeds. That's the sound of those twin overhead camshafts and four valves per cylinder – a typical modern car engine configuration. You can expect good but not flashing acceleration at motorway speeds, and reasonably sprightly getaways from traffic lights.

The acceleration figures which Land Rover gives tend to be conservative rather than optimistic, so it's worth quoting them here. Officially, then, an early 1.8-litre Freelander will hit 60mph from rest in 11.1 seconds, accelerate from 50 to 70mph in fourth (not top) gear in 10.1 seconds, and run out of steam at 102mph. As far as fuel economy is concerned, the 'combined' urban and extra-urban figure is 27.6mpg. The 2001 and later 1.8-litre models need a longer 11.8 seconds to reach 60mph but have a higher top speed of 106mph. Land Rover didn't quote a 50–70mph acceleration time. These later models are also slightly thirstier than the early ones, with a 'combined' figure of 27.3mpg.

You might like to compare these figures with the ones obtained by some of the motoring magazines (see Chapter Eight).

Drawbacks? There aren't any major ones. The 1.8-litre K-series engine has a pretty good reputation for reliability. Don't forget, though, that it has a rubber belt driving its twin overhead camshafts and that this belt must be renewed every 60,000 miles on early engines, or every 90,000 miles on the later ones. If it isn't, it can stretch or break, causing very expensive engine damage. Some people also find the 1.8-litre lacking in the performance department, and others bemoan the lack of an automatic transmission option. All the 1.8-litre Freelanders have come with the Rover PG1 five-speed manual gearbox.

There was never an automatic option with the L-series diesel engine, either. This was available between 1998 and mid-2000, and was pretty much a state-of-the-art small diesel when it was new for Rover cars back in 1994. So although it isn't the most exciting of the Freelander power units, it isn't an engine that deserves undue criticism.

All the L-series diesels deliver the same 96bhp at 4,200rpm and 155lb ft at 2,000rpm. It's quite obvious from these figures that the diesel engine doesn't rev as high as the 1.8-litre petrol type, and also that it delivers its maximum torque usefully lower down the rev range. That matters if you want to do any towing, and is a valuable asset off-road too. The engine does have an unmistakably diesel sound, but it can't be described as an unpleasant noise – and it's certainly nothing like as intrusive as most diesel engines from the 1980s or earlier.

While it's true that the L-series diesel is no ball of fire, Land Rover quotes 14.6 seconds for the 0–60mph time, a very reasonable 10.7 seconds to get from 50 to 70mph in fourth gear, and a top speed of 96mph. That's slower than the 1.8-litre K-series, admittedly, but nothing to be ashamed of. After all, how often to you want to drive faster than 96mph? Also, it is worth noting in defence of the L-series diesel that it will take a Freelander from 30 to 50mph in fourth gear in just 7.7 seconds – a whole 1.1 seconds faster than the early 1.8-litre petrol engine can manage.

The real payoff with an L-series diesel comes in its fuel economy. To quote Land Rover official figures again, you can expect 36.6mpg on the combined urban and extra-urban cycle.

However, the L-series is fairly comprehensively outclassed by the later *Td4 diesel engine*. This was

Wondering whether the Freelander you're looking at has ETC and HDC? All the 2004 models like this one do, but some early models didn't. The yellow switch here engages HDC; earlier manual models have a yellow switch on the gear lever.

designed and has always been built by BMW at that company's engine plant in the Austrian city of Steyr. Like the 1.8-litre petrol engine, it has twin overhead camshafts and four valves per cylinder, and most people who drive one for the first time have difficulty in believing that it's a diesel engine at all. It revs freely, delivers strong torque at medium and high revs as well as low revs, and only sounds like a diesel at idle.

The Td4 boasts just over 110bhp at 4,000rpm (you will hear 112 quoted for the figure, but that's actually the German PS rating), and 192lb ft of torque at 1,750rpm. While the extra power gives it some additional top-end speed as compared to the L-series diesel, what really matters is that extra torque – and the way it is delivered right the way through the rev range. There's absolutely no doubt that the Td4 is the best engine so far offered in the Freelander range (and I do include the V6 in that assessment), and it's deservedly popular. The really good news is that you can get it with either a five-speed manual gearbox (a German-made Getrag type, and not the Rover PG1 used in other Freelanders) or a five-speed automatic. The automatic – of which more in a minute – comes with Steptronic control, too.

Land Rover's figures make interesting reading. Zero to 60mph takes 13.2 seconds with the manual gearbox, or 14.3 seconds with the automatic. In both cases, it's quicker than an L-series diesel. Maximum speed is 102mph with the manual box or 100mph with the automatic – again, better than the L-series can achieve. However, these figures don't make the real point about the Td4, because they don't reveal anything about the way it goes. You'll need to test-drive one for yourself to understand that properly. And if you still need convincing when you've had a drive, remember that Land Rover's combined-cycle fuel consumption figures are 37.2mpg with the manual gearbox and 32.7mpg with the automatic.

If road performance is all you really want, then there's no alternative to the *V6 petrol engine*. Let me make the point right from the start, though, that you'll pay for your pleasure at the petrol pumps.

The V6 is a typical modern, medium-sized or executive-car power unit, with four overhead camshafts (two for each bank of the vee) operating four valves per cylinder to give optimum high-speed performance. Those four camshafts are driven by a toothed belt, which of course requires a regular but infrequent change as on all such engines to prevent problems.

In many ways, it's a delightful engine. Free-revving

and smooth, it has carefully-tuned exhaust manifolds to give quiet running at cruising speeds but an exhilarating rasp under hard acceleration. It's both powerful and torquey, too, with 175bhp at 6,250rpm and 177lb ft at 4,000rpm. Those figures make it far and away the most performance-oriented engine in the Freelander range.

Land Rover's official performance figures show just what a difference this engine makes to a Freelander. The 0 to 60mph sprint is polished off in 10.1 seconds, and maximum speed is 113mph. That's with the five-speed automatic gearbox, remember. There isn't a manual alternative (apparently for marketing reasons), which is a bit of a shame.

A manual gearbox would definitely improve on the appalling fuel consumption which drivers typically get from the V6 in its Freelander installation. Quite why it should be so bad is something Land Rover is looking into, because fuel economy in other installations (such as the Rover 800 Series cars) is quite acceptable. However, that appalling fuel consumption is one reason why the 2003 models were given a bigger fuel tank – the V6 variants simply wouldn't go far enough between fill-ups.

Officially, you'll get 22.7mpg on the combined cycle from a Freelander V6. In practice, most owners seem to struggle to reach 20mpg, and I remember hearing talk of a regular 15mpg from the drivers who were using V6 Freelanders to ferry passengers from the 2000 NEC Motor Show to Land Rover's Solihull factory where there was a special display. My own long-term loan of a Freelander V6 returned somewhere around 17mpg overall.

Which gearbox?

There's not a lot of choice here: if you want the 1.8-litre petrol or L-series diesel engines, you'll end up with a five-speed manual gearbox, come what may. If you want the V6 petrol engine, you'll have to settle for the five-speed automatic with Steptronic control. The only real choice is when you go for a Td4-powered Freelander, which allows you to choose between five-speed manual and five-speed automatic, again with Steptronic.

The 1.8-litre petrol and L-series diesel models all use the same Rover PG1 gearbox. It's a smooth-acting, inoffensive transmission, which won't bring any surprises to drivers more used to conventional cars. To drivers familiar with the heavier-feeling gearchanges in bigger and more traditional Land Rover vehicles, it will feel light and almost flimsy. This gearbox has no particular vices.

The five-speed manual used in the Td4 models isn't the same as the gearbox in the 1.8-litre and L-series Freelanders. It's a Getrag 283 gearbox, built in Germany. Although its gearchange does feel slightly more muscular than that of the PG1, it doesn't actually require any extra muscle to change gears. This is a strong, long-lasting gearbox which also doesn't have any known vices.

The five-speed automatics found in Td4 and V6 Freelanders are made by JATCO (Japanese Automatic Transmission Company), and invariably have Steptronic control. Steptronic was re-named CommandShift a couple of years after Ford took Land Rover's reins from BMW, but the two are one and the same.

What Steptronic and CommandShift allow is precise manual override of the automatic shifts. You can either leave the gearlever in its left-hand gate, when everything happens exactly as in a conventional automatic, or you can flick it over to the right, when it operates the gears manually – but of course without a clutch. Moving the gearshift forwards (to the + sign) instantly shifts up a gear, while moving it backwards (to the – sign) instantly shifts down a gear. There's an LED readout on the instrument panel so that you can't lose

All Freelanders fitted with Steptronic transmissions have ETC and HDC as standard equipment. In this case, the HDC is activated by pressing the yellow button behind the gear selector.

track of which gear you're in, and the transmission will only take over by changing up or down a gear automatically if you're about to do something silly – such as overspeeding the engine or making it labour unnecessarily. It sounds much more complicated than it is, and in fact it's a delight to use.

Where to look

If you're going to buy a used Freelander, you'll find that many local used-car dealers simply won't touch them, because they see them as a specialist vehicle. However, used Freelanders are by no means hard to find. Try a specialist 4x4 dealer, the classified ads (especially in the 4x4 magazines), or a Land Rover franchised dealership.

It should be no surprise to discover that the most expensive vehicles will be on the forecourts of the franchised dealers. This isn't just because they will generally be fairly recent examples, either: Land Rover dealers have to put a lot of their own money into making their premises conform to Land Rover's corporate scheme, and they have to claw it back somehow.

Next down in price will be Freelanders at specialist 4x4 dealerships. Newer ones are likely to be just as good as comparable examples at a franchised dealership, and they will be rather cheaper. Some dealerships offer insurance-type warranties, and a good one of these is worth having. You'll discover whether the warranty is likely to be any good or not by reading the small print before you sign up.

Cheapest of the lot will be vehicles sold privately through classified ads. The seller knows he can get more from you than he'll get by selling to a dealer (who has to show a profit on the re-sale); but his price is likely to be well below that which a dealer will charge. Of course, you get no warranty, and so you'll have to take that much more care to satisfy yourself that the vehicle is sound in every respect. That also means you need to take care that you're not buying a stolen vehicle or one on which there is still finance outstanding. The best bet here is to contact one of the specialist agencies, who will run a check on your behalf for a relatively modest fee. In the UK, try the AA Used Car Data Check (Tel: 0870 600 0838; web site: www.theaa.com), the RAC (Tel: 0870 533 3660; web site: www.rac.co.uk) or HPI Equifax (Tel: 01722 413434; web site: www.hpicheck.com).

The bad news for buyers is that Freelanders are still holding their value well, though you can expect that situation to change when the second-generation model is released in the mid-2000s. So take a look at as many

advertisements as you can, and get a feel for average prices. Don't forget that prices may vary in different parts of the country. When you're sure that you know what's a reasonable price for the model you want, start checking a few out. Suspiciously cheap isn't automatically bad news – it may be a distress sale where the owner needs the money fast – but you should take extra care in such cases that you're not buying a stolen vehicle or a rebuilt write-off, and that there isn't something terminally wrong with the vehicle which will cost you a lot to put right.

What goes wrong?

What, then, are the things you should look for when buying a used Freelander? It's pleasing to be able to report that the junior Land Rover hasn't revealed very many major problems five-and-a-bit years into its showroom life. However, that isn't to say that it won't do as the years and the miles mount up. Nor can I say that the vehicle is without its faults.

Despite BMW's best efforts to get the Freelander assembly facility up to its own very high standards, it's a fact that Land Rover's traditionally iffy build quality did carry over to the Freelander. Perhaps there have been fewer problem Freelanders than there were rogue Discoverys in the mid-1990s, but it's a fact that dealers have been kept fairly busy carrying out warranty work on Freelanders.

For a list of early problems, have another look at Chapter Four. Water leaks into the vehicle, squeaks from seats and trim, and poor detail finish have remained intermittent problems on new Freelanders right up to the present day. When checking a used vehicle after purchase, don't be tempted to scrape away that line of mastic which appears to be there for no reason: it was probably applied under warranty to cure a wind whistle or water leak!

There have been many problems associated with the driveline, perhaps because the elements of the system – which has an unusual configuration – need to be set up with more care than is sometimes taken. One recurrent problem has been a fractured or broken IRD support bracket on 1.8-litre petrol models, which generally shows up as a vibration when the engine is running at about 4,000rpm. There have also been problems with the differentials at both ends of the car, with the bearings between the differentials and the IRD (again at both ends), and with wheel bearings, especially at the rear.

A persistent problem with pre-2001 vehicles was

HOW OLD IS THAT VEHICLE YOU'RE LOOKING AT?

A look at the VIN number (visible through the bottom of the black windscreen surround on the left-hand side) will tell you instantly the model-year of your vehicle. This is not necessarily the same as the calendar year in which it was built. The Land Rover model-year runs from autumn to autumn, and so vehicles built in October 2000 and June 2001 are both 2001 models as far as Land Rover is concerned.

It should go without saying that the VIN on the vehicle must match that on the vehicle registration document (V5 in the UK). If it doesn't, suspect dirty work and don't buy!

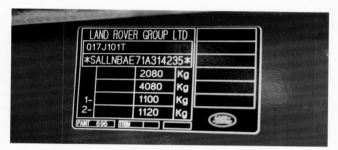

You can identify when a Freelander was built by checking its VIN code. Lists are given in earlier chapters of this book, and a look at Chapter Five will reveal that this vehicle is a 2001 model-year Freelander Commercial with the Td4 engine.

The full details of Freelander VIN codes are given in Chapters Four to Six, but for convenience here's a list of the model-year codes. They are always contained in the last-but-one digit of the alphanumeric prefix to the six-digit serial number.

W =	1998 model-year	1 =	2001 model-year
X =	1999 model-year	2 =	2002 model-year
Y =	2000 model-year	3 =	2003 model-year

In Britain since the 1960s, elements of the registration number have also revealed the approximate date when a vehicle was new. When you're looking at advertisements for used Freelanders, you might well find that a vehicle's age is given only in terms of its registration number. So below is a list of the registration codes which will help you date a vehicle for sale.

Don't rely on this evidence alone: check the VIN code to see when the vehicle was built as well. It's possible, for example, that a Freelander built in mid-1999 wasn't registered until the 2000-season registrations were in use. That doesn't make it a 2000 model, whatever the seller will tell you!

While a vehicle may carry a 'cherished' number which was issued before its date of first registration, British law does not permit vehicles to be re-registered with later numbers which make them appear newer than they are.

The table below will help you establish a registration date for any used vehicle you are looking at. R212 BAC was in fact an early Land Rover press demonstrator, dating from the 1998 model-year . . .

. . . and while LR51 XYZ may be a dummy plate, it illustrates the type of registration number used between 1 September 2001 and 28 February 2002.

Letter prefix codes (eg, R212 BDU)

R	1 August 1997 to 31 July 1998
S	1 August 1998 to 28 February 1999
T	1 March 1999 to 31 August 1999
V	1 September 1999 to 28 February 2000
W	1 March 2000 to 31 August 2000
X	1 September 2000 to 28 February 2001
Y	1 March 2001 to 31 August 2001

Numerical codes (eg, BV52 KGJ)

51	1 September 2001 to 28 February 2002
02	1 March 2002 to 31 August 2002
52	1 September 2002 to 28 February 2003
03	1 March 2003 to 31 August 2003
53	1 September 2003 to 28 February 2004

. . . and so on.

excessive rear tyre wear. Not every vehicle was affected, but some owners (especially outside the UK, it appears) returned again and again to their dealerships, only to be told that there was no problem and that the fault must lie in the way they used the vehicle.

Land Rover has always kept the lid very tightly on this issue, and so it's impossible at present to confirm the stories that some early IRD units did not live up to their design specification. In a nutshell, it appears that they allowed the rear tyres to scrub, so wearing the tread. However, the fact that Land Rover changed the specification of the IRD on 2001 models and again on 2002 models – and that the problems still persist – does tend to point to the accuracy of those stories! Watch out, then, for rear tyres which are significantly more worn than the fronts; they are likely to indicate that the IRD problem is present.

Unfortunately, the IRD is a sealed unit and early units cannot be modified to the later specification. Therefore, if you suspect a faulty IRD on an early vehicle, the only remedy is to change the whole unit for one of the later types. Sadly, it won't be cheap, and it won't necessarily cure the problem.

Although the diesel engines are largely problem-free, the petrol engines have given trouble in service. This is surprising, as all the K-series derivatives have proved durable and reliable in their car applications. On early 1.8-litre engines, the plastic throttle mechanism can break, while all 1.8-litre types can suffer from burned pistons and from blown head gaskets.

On the V6 engines, the baffles in the plastic exhaust manifold can come loose and rattle when the engine is under power. As the manifold is a sealed unit, it must be replaced rather than repaired, and this is an

A weakness of the 1.8-litre K-series lies in its head gasket's proneness to leak. Driving with a blown gasket and a boiling engine can lead to extensive damage.

expensive job. Some V6 engines have also developed a persistent misfire, which has been followed by the head gasket blowing around No. 4 cylinder. In some cases, the associated damage has been so severe that Land Rover has authorised replacement engines under warranty. Although most cases of this will have been rectified under warranty, there may still be some problems waiting to happen in low-mileage engines.

The PG1 five-speed gearboxes used with the 1.8-litre petrol and L-series diesel engines have also had their share of problems, although the Getrag five-speeder used behind the Td4 diesel seems to be problem-free.

Another potential problem area is the Softback on models so equipped. Some owners refuse to read the instructions about how to use it before they try to do so, with the result that the fabric can become damaged. On all Softback models, it's advisable to check that the mechanism does work smoothly and that neither the windows nor the fabric have become damaged from misuse or vandalism. Later models (from VIN 208990 in the 2002 model-year) have minor modifications to the softback.

It is also worth checking the bodies of the rear lamp units in the bumper. In cases where an exhaust failure which has been left unrepaired has allowed hot gases to get into the bumper void, the heat has distorted the lamp body and, in extreme cases, the bumper itself. The wiring harness may also have been damaged.

On the tail door, it is worth checking the upper corners for corrosion, where rough finish has not allowed the protective paint coating to adhere properly. There have also been many cases of water leaks through tail doors, in particular because of a rubber seal which has split.

Finally, heaters have been known to give trouble (so check carefully that heat is delivered as it should be), and front suspension links can sometimes break, although probably only when a Freelander has been subjected to abuse such as heavy kerbing.

A few final thoughts

It should be obvious, really, but when you're buying a used Freelander, don't let the raft of accessories which its last owner put on influence your choice unduly. They may be very nearly exactly what you want, but it's no use having a set of nifty alloy wheels and some chrome side runners if you're just about to need a new set of tyres or there's a suspicious misfire. Accessories can always be added later – when you're sure that everything else is working as Solihull intended.

Personalising the Freelander

Making yours more your own

It was inevitable that as mass production delivered ever greater quantities of cars which looked the same, so customers would seek ways of making their cars look different from all the others parked in their neighbours' drives. In the USA, manufacturers exploited this in the 1950s by offering a range of subtly different derivatives of the same design, and the practice reached the UK in the early 1960s with the 'badge-engineered' models produced by the British Motor Corporation and the Rootes Group.

Gradually, the business of offering myriad variations on a theme became a science. And so when Land Rover planned to sell its new Discovery in larger volumes than any previous model, it made sure that every buyer would be able to personalise his or her vehicle to a very great extent. No fewer than 50 different accessory options were available at the vehicle's launch in 1989, in addition to all the traditional permutations of engine type, body colour, and so on.

Land Rover offered a wide variety of options for the Freelander from Day One. This 1999-model 50th Anniversary three-door Softback came packed with them as standard. Visible here are the side mouldings, headlamp guards, bright metal side runners, 17-inch Triple Sport alloy wheels, apron-mounted driving lamps, A-bar with additional lamps, and roof rails.

By the time the Freelander went on sale nine years later, the market expected even more. As Land Rover intended to sell the Freelander in even greater numbers than the Discovery, it was that much more important for buyers to be able to individualise their vehicles. So a range of 100 accessories – twice as many as at the Discovery launch – was made available for Freelander buyers right from the start. That number has since increased and, of course, the activities of aftermarket accessory manufacturers have provided Freelander owners with an even wider variety of options for personalising their vehicles.

It is very easy to spend a small fortune on accessories when you're buying a brand-new Freelander from a Land Rover dealer. It's also very tempting to spend a lot of money on freshening up an older model bought second-hand: some shiny new alloy wheels can make a Freelander look like new again, and a couple more additions to the original specification can make it seem more luxurious than the way it was when it left the factory. There's really no end to what you can do – except, perhaps, when your bank manager's patience runs out.

So it is a good idea to spend your money wisely on accessorising and personalising your Freelander. One of the most important things to remember, though, is that most accessories do not add value to the vehicle and that you won't recoup what you've spent when you come to sell it. At most, your well-accessorised vehicle may sell rather faster than a similarly priced one without all the extras. If you want accessories, then, make sure that they are of real value to you personally.

To help you decide how you might want to personalise your Freelander, I've divided the range of accessories into broad categories. Both Land Rover's own accessories and aftermarket types are included, and – as the range of aftermarket add-ons is increasing all the time – I'm not going to pretend that these categories offer any kind of definitive listing. What they do aim to do, though, is to give you ideas for what you might want to do with your Freelander to make it fit your needs better.

Good luck, and spend wisely!

Exterior decoration

Most people seem to start on personalising a vehicle by making some distinctive changes to the outside. That way, it's easier to recognise their own vehicles in car parks filled with similar ones . . .

There are many different ways you can do this on a Freelander. Frankly, the most useful exterior additions are the side rubbing-strips available through Land Rover. They are made of rubber and are designed to absorb minor parking knocks (such as when a car door is opened against the side of your vehicle). Some people insist on having them painted to match the bodywork of their Freelanders, which may look good but means that the chipped paintwork from a parking nudge is on the rubbing-strip rather than the main bodywork: you still have to touch-in the damage. It's sensible advice to fit them in their natural black rubber state and leave them that way.

Another way of protecting the flanks of your Freelander from minor damage is to fit the bright steel 'protection bars' from Land Rover. These fit along the side sills under the doors and will ward off some attacks from carelessly opened doors in a car park, but to be honest, their main function is cosmetic.

Land Rover offers body styling kits for both the three-door and five-door Freelanders, and these are quite different to suit the different characters of the two models. The three-door styling kit consists of tubular strakes which are added to the vehicle's flanks and are matched by wheelarch extensions. This kit was actually standard on the 50th Anniversary three-door models in 1998, when it was finished in the body colour – but it's possible to paint it to contrast with the body, of course. For the five-door, the styling kit is deliberately more practical, and consists of additional plastic protection panels along the lower edge of the body sides and doors; typically, these are left unpainted, to match the wheelarches and the front and rear bumper aprons.

Body graphics (side decals) were introduced when the Freelander first went on sale, and in the UK have not proved popular. They are purely cosmetic; don't let anyone con you into thinking they protect anything. While they may well protect the paintwork against stone chips, they will chip and scratch themselves – and then you're looking at quite a large bill to replace them. For the 2000 model-year, the original graphics were changed for a more stylish set called 'Blue Waves', which certainly give an attractive appearance to the rather slab-sided five-door models.

Wrap-around bull-bars are available for the Freelander, although they are frowned upon by the European Community and Land Rover no longer offers them in the UK. This bright steel example was fitted to a Freelander at the Montreal Motor Show in 2001 where it was pictured by Kevin Girling. Light guards and a roof-mounted mountain bike rack are also in evidence.

**15" STYLED
STEEL WHEEL**

**15" ADVENTURE
ALLOY WHEEL**

**16" FREEDOM 5 SPOKE
ALLOY WHEEL**

**16" ACTIVE
ALLOY WHEEL**

**16" TRIPLE SPORT
ALLOY WHEEL**

**17" FREEDOM 6 SPOKE
ALLOY WHEEL
(ACCESSORY FIT ONLY)**

**17" TREK
ALLOY WHEEL**

**17" EVOLUTION
ALLOY WHEEL**

**17" TRIPLE SPORT
ALLOY WHEEL
(ACCESSORY FIT ONLY)**

Also allegedly designed to protect your vehicle are several different types of frontal armour. These have their design roots in roo-bars – great metal constructions added to the front of 4x4s used in the Australian Outback. In Australia, they had (and still have) a real value, because kangaroos tend to jump in front of a moving vehicle without warning and the resulting collision does nearly as much damage to the vehicle as to the luckless kangaroo. 'Roo-bars were designed to protect the vulnerable radiator from damage, so that the vehicle could still keep going in an area where there was no chance of finding water to top-up a leaking cooling system. When they reached Europe and the USA as a styling accessory, they were generally known as 'bull-bars' because there were clearly no 'roos around to need protection from.

Land Rover introduced frontal protection for the Freelander right from the start, with A-frame 'nudge bars' in stainless steel or black, and a more pedestrian-friendly black 'front protection bar' with a flexible outer covering. When the European Commission drew attention in 2001 to the damage that bull-bars could do to pedestrians hit by a moving vehicle, the company withdrew its rigid A-frames from the market. Nevertheless, Freelander bull-bars can still be bought through many aftermarket outlets. It's questionable whether they have any value whatsoever beyond the macho look which some people believe they confer on a vehicle – unless you do a lot of driving in the Australian Outback, of course.

Flying stones can of course crack headlamp lenses, and so Land Rover offers clear acrylic lens shields – and there are some available to protect the optional fog lamps as well. These, though, are more practical than cosmetic. Buyers generally prefer the metal slat-type lens protectors which actually don't do the job as well as the acrylic shields but do look tough. These can be matched by similar 'lamp protectors' for the lamps in the rear body pillars and the lamps in the rear bumper. Aftermarket makers offer these, as do Land Rover.

Lastly, the tail end of a Freelander can be enhanced by a cover over the spare wheel. These items are popular: they keep road dirt off the spare wheel so that it remains more pleasant to handle when needed, and they also discourage light-fingered individuals from

attempting to steal your valuable alloy wheel with its brand-new tyre attached. A lot of Land Rover and other 4x4 dealers also give them away free when selling a vehicle, as they offer an ideal opportunity for advertising their business!

Land Rover offers three main types: a rigid one with black centre and bright metal rim; an all-black styled type in ABS plastic which picks up the strakes motif used on the three-door body styling kit; and a black vinyl type with the Land Rover logo in a colour which only vaguely resembles the green Land Rover approved back in 1988. There are also many aftermarket offerings, and some specialist companies will apply your own personal design to a wheel cover.

However, not all spare wheel covers were created equal. The rigid types are hardest-wearing and, of course, most expensive. The all-vinyl types are the cheapest – and some of those available are cheap in every sense of the word, so check carefully what you're buying. Remember, too, that a spare wheel cover designed to fit over a narrow tyre on a 15-inch wheel may not fit very well over a wider tyre on a 17-inch wheel, so changing your wheel-and-tyre combination might necessitate a wheel cover change as well.

Wheels and tyres

As I've noted above, fitting a set of new alloy wheels to an older vehicle can make it look fresher, and is a favourite among Freelander buyers. Land Rover has offered a big variety of different wheel-and-tyre combinations for its junior model over the years, and to get some idea of what is available you can take a look at the list relating to the 2002 models in Chapter Six and the illustration opposite. There are also some aftermarket alloy wheels available for Freelanders.

It's commonly accepted that bigger wheels, with correspondingly shallower tyres, look more attractive than small wheels with tall tyres. That being so, it's also common practice to charge more for bigger wheels (because they're bigger) than for small ones, and more for the tyres to go on them (because they supposedly have a more complex construction). So a new set of alloy wheels with appropriate tyres might cost you a lot more than you expect.

Some people try to save money by buying only four new wheels and tyres, and leaving a serviceable older wheel-and-tyre on the spare, which is then concealed under a spare wheel cover. This is all very well if the new wheels and tyres are the same size as the old, but in many instances they aren't. It can be dangerous (and

There is a bewildering variety of wheel options for the Freelander. This illustration comes from a 2002 model-year sales brochure, and puts names to the various styles available through Land Rover. Steel ones are the best bet for off-roading!

Not everybody's cup of tea, perhaps – but these twin lighting pods were made available as an accessory through Land Rover for the V6 models.

PERSONAL EXPERIENCE

The author of this book is no stranger to the business of modifying and personalising a Land Rover product. Between 1987 and 2001, I ran a 1974 Range Rover as an everyday vehicle, gradually personalising it to create what I wanted.

This well-known Range Rover (which has been featured in several magazines) started life as a 1974-model two-door in Tuscan Blue with a four-speed manual gearbox and V8 petrol engine. By the time I decided to sell it on, it had become a four-door in Cassis Red metallic with a four-speed automatic gearbox and an uprated 200 Tdi diesel engine. It had also been fitted with air conditioning, a mid-1980s Vogue-specification interior and a host of other items such as a CD player.

Why did I sell it on? Simply because the further modifications I wanted were not practical. It was not possible to add ABS or airbags – both desirable safety features which I wanted to have in the family car after the birth of my son.

And there's a lesson in there for Freelander owners: ABS and airbags are not items which you can add to a Freelander which doesn't have them, either. So if you think you'll ever want these features, make sure you start with a Freelander which already has ABS (which comes with HDC and ETC) and a passenger's side airbag (a driver's side airbag was always standard)!

in many countries is definitely illegal) to fit that odd-sized spare, even in an emergency.

If you're planning to use your Freelander a lot off-road, it's worth reading through the section below devoted to off-road modifications before you decide to buy a new set of wheels and tyres.

As a final thought on wheels and tyres, don't forget that Land Rover offers some purpose-designed quick-release tyre chains for Freelanders used in snowy areas.

Additional lighting

Right from the beginning, additional lighting for the Freelander has been available through Land Rover. Fairly rare have always been the foglamps which were mounted in pods into the face of the front apron; for some reason, these did not catch the buying public's imagination.

However, driving lamps mounted either ahead of the radiator air intake (Land Rover supplied Safari 3000 items with detachable stoneguards) or in pods on the bumper alongside the front numberplate were much better appreciated. These pods incorporated either a single lamp on each side or, for the V6 models with their differently profiled bumper and apron, twin lamps on each side.

If you want some additional driving lamps, you obviously don't have to buy them through Land Rover. There are many perfectly good proprietary brands on the market which will do the job just as well. Take my advice, though: make sure the ones you buy have detachable stoneguards because flying stones thrown up by other vehicles will very quickly crack the exposed lenses if you don't.

Recently, it's been possible to buy aftermarket replacement headlamp bulbs which give the blue-tinted light associated with the gas-discharge headlamps used on some expensive modern cars. Some types are also rated at a higher wattage than the standard Freelander lamps, and there are some which give a very blue light – designed more for effect than anything else and in some cases, actually illegal for road use. Take advice before buying, and choose carefully. Remember, too, that the standard Freelander headlamps are in no sense inadequate.

It is also possible to update the appearance of an early Freelander with the clear indicator lenses used on 2001 and later models. It's a relatively inexpensive way of giving your Freelander a facelift – but you won't fool an expert into thinking the vehicle is newer than it really is!

Seating and comfort

You'll spend a lot of time sitting in your Freelander and looking at its interior features, and to be honest, you would be well advised to make sure you have this part of the vehicle personalised to your taste before you worry about the outside.

Worth thinking about then, are various appliqué kits for the dash. Land Rover offers an aluminium-effect kit and a similar kit in attractive Hunter Green, which will add a touch of distinction to the part of the Freelander you'll be looking at most. Various aftermarket suppliers also offer appliqué wood kits, which certainly add an impression of luxury. Don't be tempted to go for the cheapest you can find, though: in a worst case, the fake wood can chip or peel away from the plastic fascia underneath.

Freelander seats are pretty supportive and comfortable, but there's no doubt that the 'premium' seats introduced for the 2002 model-year and standardised for 2004 offer greater comfort than the standard type. No Freelander seats yet offer an inboard armrest for the front seat occupants, and that's a major omission in my view. If you want such armrests on your Freelander, you'll need to speak to a trimming specialist

(such as Nationwide Trim in the UK, Tel: 01527 518851) to see what can be done. For the outboard armrests (on the door trims), Land Rover itself offers some very worthwhile pads which make these items much more comfortable to use.

Now that Land Rover has withdrawn its Autobiography service for Freelanders, you will have to go to an aftermarket specialist if you want a major change to the interior of your vehicle. Most trimming specialists can offer a variety of services, but with a little perseverance it's possible to find one who can undertake a high-quality transformation which makes the factory-issue interior seem very dowdy indeed. A surprisingly affordable makeover of this type is available from The Seat Surgeons (Tel: 01347 811481) – who are used by Land Rover main dealers in the York area to upgrade vehicles for customers.

You don't have to go quite that far with your Freelander's interior, of course. Both Land Rover and some aftermarket specialists sell waterproof seat covers which will protect what you already have and can look

Wood trim kits and leather upholstery can make a big difference to the overall feel of a Freelander's interior.

The leather upholstery options on Freelanders have always been relatively sober. However, high-quality re-trims are available from companies such as The Seat Surgeons (Tel: 01347 811481) who re-trimmed a five-door Station Wagon in this striking red and black scheme. It also includes an add-on imitation wood kit.

quite stylish into the bargain. Then there are of course carpet mats for the footwells in a variety of colours as well as more utilitarian rubber mats. Both Land Rover dealers and aftermarket specialists offer a choice.

Many people nowadays would argue that air conditioning is an essential for any car, and in many countries around the world it certainly is. My own experience teaches me that once you've had a car with air conditioning you will never want one without it: even in the cold and wet UK it has far more value than I'd have believed before I got used to it. It's possible to add air conditioning to a Freelander which doesn't have it, as the basic vehicle was designed to accommodate it. However, get an expert to do it (the gases used in the system are harmful) and don't expect it to be cheap.

Convenience and practicality

By far the largest range of accessories for the Freelander is designed to meet the twin aims of convenience and practicality. Land Rover itself has most of the bases covered here, but aftermarket suppliers are also getting in on the act.

Different people carry different things in their Freelanders, and there's a big range of accessories to tailor the vehicle to some quite precise requirements. For the rear loadspace, you can buy a simple ribbed rubber floor mat or a rigid loadspace liner. Various luggage nets can be had to keep things tidily stacked against the sides of the load bay, and there's even an insert for the undefloor stowage box to keep things tidy in there.

Right: Another variation on the front A-bar is seen on this South African Freelander pictured by Tim Race during the annual dealer-team TReK competition. Note also the roof rack, secured by mountings within the roof itself.

There are dog guards to keep the pooch out of the passenger cabin, too, and there's a rigid loadspace cover for the three-door and a roller-blind type for the five-door to conceal your shopping from light-fingered onlookers. (If you've left the Softback at home and it starts to rain, you can also fit a showerproof cover over the rear of a three-door, and that's an item worth having.)

Not all Freelanders have roof rails as standard, and it's possible to retro-fit them to either five-door or three-door models. On the latter, they come with stylish bracing bars which run down the back of the body on either side. You can buy cross-bars for these roof rails, which turn them into a simple (but not very strong) roof rack.

If a roof rack is what you really want, there's a basket-type luggage carrier which mounts to the roof rails. Or, if you want a full-length roof rack which looks good as well, talk to Safety Devices who designed a very neat one for the Freelanders used in the 2003 G4 Challenge (see Chapter Nine). The standard roof rails can also be fitted with a lockable box made by world-renowned manufacturer Thule, with a lockable ski-box, with a simple exposed ski-rack or with a single-bicycle rack. There's even a sailboard carrier with a mastholder and quick-release strap, and for Commercial variants, there is a whole range of pipe carriers, ladder racks and the like which fit to the standard roof rails.

If you want to carry more than one bicycle, then you'll need a special carrier mounted on the tow bar (and you'll have to fit a tow bar, too, of course – there are lots of different types on offer). Also available for mounting to the spare wheel carrier is a range of carrying devices manufactured by Hitchlugger in the UK, and among them is an alternative bike carrier.

Freelanders are higher off the ground than most ordinary cars, and shorter people sometimes find that it's a struggle to get on board. Available both from Land Rover and aftermarket suppliers are side steps (some varieties are called 'side runners') which alleviate this problem at a stroke. It's worth knowing that these can offer additional protection against minor car park knocks and that they can compromise the vehicle's off-road ability because they hang down below the body. Buy good, solid ones from a reputable manufacturer. Cheap side steps invariably look like what they are, and in some cases their fixings can be suspect, too.

A couple of other items deserve mention here. Very practical indeed are the front and rear mud flaps

available from Land Rover, which help to keep road dirt off the sides of your Freelander. And, if you like driving with all the windows open, you might like to think about the clear acrylic wind deflectors which fit around the tops and leading edges of the window openings and keep draughts at bay.

More performance or more economy?

Many owners decide that standard engine tunes aren't for them; what they want is a go-faster Freelander.

There are several aftermarket companies who can deliver the goods in this department. For high-performance diesel engines, the accepted methods of tuning are to re-chip the electronic management system and/or (usually and) to add a bigger intercooler. For a few hundred pounds, it's therefore possible to get better on-road performance out of your diesel Freelander.

For high-performance petrol engines, a rechip of the management system can again do the trick. Beware of losing low-down torque if you plan to do much off-roading, as some rechips will effectively move the torque band further up the rev scale so that better acceleration is available from high speeds, but bottom-end torque is thus affected.

No doubt it's possible also to get extra performance from the Freelander's petrol engines by fitting turbochargers or superchargers – and the latter is exactly what Callaway did for the concept vehicle they built for Land Rover North America (see Chapter Seven). However, at the time of writing, such conversions are not widely available.

However, there are a few things to know before you get started. First, tuned engines don't necessarily have shorter life-spans than standard ones, but it's common sense that the greater the stresses to which you subject an engine, the faster it may wear. If you always drive a tuned Freelander very hard, you may find that you reduce the life of some of its engine components.

Secondly, it is possible to get quite a lot more power and torque out of an engine if you disregard the emissions requirements which many countries now have in force. Before getting your performance increase, find out whether what's on offer will break the law.

Thirdly, there's rarely any gain without a little pain. The rechipped Td4 Freelander which Land Rover offered German customers (see Chapter Six) was noticeably more thirsty than the standard article. Most tuned engines are likely to use more fuel than non-tuned ones unless you drive them gently – and if you're going to do that, why have your engine performance-tuned in the first place?

If it's not better acceleration you want, but better fuel economy, you don't have much choice with the diesel engines except to go easy with your right foot. For petrol engines, though, it's worth considering an LPG conversion. In many countries, LPG (liquefied petroleum gas) is considerably cheaper to buy than ordinary petrol, so the fact that it usually delivers slightly poorer fuel economy is amply offset by the gains.

At the time of writing, Land Rover was said to be working on an approved, bolt-on LPG conversion for the V6 engine, and one for the 1.8-litre types would follow if the demand justified it. In this context, it is important to remember that not everybody who claims to offer an LPG conversion works to the same high standards – and that's why Land Rover has taken an interest in giving official approval to add-on systems. If you're not sure about the credentials of the LPG converters you have in mind, check to see if they belong to the LPGA (LP Gas Association). Membership is a guarantee of quality.

Are there drawbacks to LPG? Availability of the fuel is nowhere near as good as availability of petrol (although it is said to be improving all the time), so make sure you won't have to drive 20 miles to find somewhere to fill up. There's also the fact that you will need to find somewhere to put the special LPG tank on your vehicle – and this can eat up space in a compact 4x4 like the Freelander. Most LPG-fuelled vehicles retain the ability to run on petrol as well, which means that you actually need two fuel tanks – one for the LPG and the second, usually a small, reserve tank, for the petrol.

Sheer indulgence

Some people might say that a great deal of what you can buy to personalise your Freelander qualifies for this section on 'sheer indulgence', but this isn't the place to pursue that argument!

Under this heading, then, let's include the items that very few people really need, but plenty of people would like to have. Upgrading your Freelander's ICE system definitely qualifies here, as even the one fitted to entry-level models gives quite reasonable performance (unless you're deaf or always drive with the windows open).

You can upgrade by using the system fitted to more expensive versions of the Freelander, or you can go to an ICE specialist and spend as much money as you choose. Don't forget that top-model Freelanders now come with a superb Harman Kardon branded system which includes a remotely mounted six-CD stacker. You're unlikely to need anything much better than that, and it's already tailor-made to fit your vehicle. The downside is that it's expensive.

Fitting a satellite navigation system must also qualify here. Land Rover does offer a system (which differs from country to country) but it's not as good as the one offered in the Range Rover (for example). The biggest obstacle to a satisfactory satnav system in the Freelander is that there's nowhere to site the monitor screen neatly. Your best bet will probably be to visit an aftermarket specialist, but don't expect to get away with a cheap installation.

More and more people these days expect driving aids such as a parking sensor at the rear, and it's possible to

Park Distance Control is Land Rover's name for parking aids in the rear bumper, but there are aftermarket versions available, too.

install one of these in your Freelander. I've included this as a 'sheer indulgence' because a Freelander isn't a difficult vehicle to park – for most people. However, if you do want one of these ultrasonic devices which bleeps insistently to warn you that you're about to reverse into something, then make sure you get a good one. I'd recommend one which has four sensors rather than the two which some manufacturers suggest are adequate for the job.

What else could you possibly want? Well, if you have a three-door Freelander with the original 'plastic' targa roof panels, you might want to replace these with the opaque glass panels. Then you'll probably want the roller blinds which fit underneath these so that you can block out bright light . . .

Going the off-road route

As Chapter Nine makes clear, there's a great deal of fun to be had from using a Freelander off-road. The more you get into off-roading, however, the more you will recognise that certain items which didn't come as standard on your Freelander would improve things.

Let's start with wheels and tyres. The attractive alloy wheels on your Freelander won't stay attractive for too long if they get scraped by rocks and tree-stumps when you drive off-road. They are made of a relatively soft alloy, and the first thing you'll notice is that the protective surface gets scratched off (just as it does when you hit the kerb in city driving). Next, the alloy itself may begin to corrode, and little patches of bubbled-up metal around a smart alloy wheel soon stop it from looking smart. In fact, a scruffy alloy wheel looks very down-market indeed.

That's when you'll discover that the alloy wheels are expensive to replace. So your best bet, if you plan to continue using your Freelander off-road, is to replace the alloys with a set of the 15-inch styled steel wheels used on entry-level Freelanders. They might not be as attractive as the alloys, but they are more hard-wearing, they can more easily be tidied up (a quick spray with silver paint usually does a good, if temporary, job) and they are nowhere near as expensive. If your budget runs to it, have a set of smart alloys for road use and a set of steel wheels on off-road tyres for off-road use.

Chapter Nine also pointed out that there isn't a very wide choice of dedicated off-road tyres for the Freelander as yet, although the position is changing.

Freelanders were used on the G4 Challenge marketing exercise in 2003. North America subsequently had a limited-edition G4 Challenge Freelander model. (Nick Dimbleby)

The standard tyres will soon clog with mud, so you do want to get something a little more specialised if you intend to do a lot of off-road driving. The best bet for the moment is likely to be a 'Mud and Snow' tyre, which has a more aggressive tread pattern and will, as its name suggests, cope with both mud and snow.

However, introduced in 2003 was a new tyre from Goodyear called the Wrangler MT/R, which was used on the Freelanders that took part in the 2003 Land Rover G4 Challenge. The indications are that it will be expensive when it goes on public sale, but the word from experts within Land Rover is that it is a superb off-road tyre which is also very good on the road. It is unlikely to be the last of its kind, as other tyre manufacturers begin to appreciate that they can sell off-road tyres in this size.

One of the Freelander's handicaps in off-road use is its relative lack of ground clearance. One way of getting around this is to fit taller tyres, although it's important to remember that this is likely to require other modifications as well. Bigger tyres may raise the vehicle further off the ground, but they may also foul the wheelarches under certain conditions. There are two ways of getting around this. One is to modify the wheelarches by cutting them away to give the necessary

clearance. The other is to raise the whole vehicle on its suspension. You'll need to talk to specialists about this (find one through the pages of the 4x4 magazines) because you will need not only longer springs but dampers (shock absorbers) with longer travel as well.

That lack of ground clearance makes the Freelander's underside prone to damage, and the standard 'bash-plate' which protects the steering and front protection is a tacit admission of the fact. However, the transverse rear silencer remains vulnerable. Camel Trophy Freelanders (see Chapter Nine) had a specially constructed protective frame to take the knocks while leaving the silencer accessible in case it needed to be changed. For the G4 Challenge vehicles (again, see Chapter Nine), Mantec Services developed a whole range of specialist equipment which included tougher front-end protection and a silencer guard plate. These, like the other special items developed for the G4 Freelanders, are were due to go on public sale during 2003.

The Mantec items will certainly be followed by others in the same vein, but as a range of off-road accessories

The Camel Trophy adventure competition probably proved more about the Freelander's off-road abilities than the G4 Challenge did. (Nick Dimbleby)

Properly equipped for the job, the Freelander makes a formidable off-roader, as this French vehicle demonstrated at the Belgium National event in 2002. It is equipped with a wide variety of aftermarket accessories.

they do compensate very well for the Freelander's weak points off-road. They include strong underbody sills (which allow the vehicle to be lifted securely by a high-lifting jack), a purpose-designed engine breather snorkel (to aid deep-water wading), front and rear light guards (to protect the lenses from flying stones or tough branches), and receiver points at front and rear for a demountable winch.

There is one other item you should consider if you intend to do any really heavy-duty off-roading with your Freelander, and that is a roll cage. Companies such as Safety Devices in the UK can advise you on what is needed – but bear in mind that this is a serious off-roader's accessory and not a macho-look add-on. A roll cage is designed to strengthen the vehicle's body so that if it falls on to its roof, this will not cave in. It is usually fitted inside the passenger compartment, and will be a tubular structure which occupies valuable space. Most are not demountable, being welded firmly into position to afford as much extra body strength as possible.

. . . and lastly

Land Rover really hasn't missed a trick in the accessories department. You can usually buy the items in this final section more cheaply elsewhere, but if you really must get them from your Land Rover dealership, you can order two different types of baby seat, a booster seat, a warning triangle, a foot pump, a set of tyre pressure and tread depth gauges, a fire extinguisher, a first aid kit and a hand lamp.

One thing you can't get anywhere else (as far as I know) is a device which Land Rover calls a cool-hot box. Electrically operated, it plugs into the cigarette lighter (or the auxiliary power socket if one is fitted) and operates as a fridge or – at the flick of a switch – will keep your food warm instead.

Index